P9-DDN-594

NATIONAL
GEOGRAPHIC
KiDS

Absolute Expert

DINOSAURS

All the
LATEST
FACTS From
the Field

Lela Nargi

**With National Geographic Explorer
Steve Brusatte**

3 1150 01623 5265

**NATIONAL GEOGRAPHIC
Washington, D.C.**

BOISE PUBLIC LIBRARY

CONTENTS

CHAPTER 2
Here Come the Dinosaurs 32

CHAPTER 1
Superstars of the Mesozoic Era 8

CHAPTER 3
The Lives of Dinosaurs 60

CHAPTER 4
After the Dinosaurs 84

STEVE BRUSATTE

STEVE EXAMINES A ROCK CONTAINING A MARINE REPTILE FOSSIL ON THE ISLE OF EIGG, SCOTLAND.

When I was a kid, I wasn't interested in science at all. In fact, it was my least favorite class in school! I wasn't bad at it, and I didn't dread it. I was just much more into social studies.

It wasn't until I was about 14 years old, in my first year of high school, that I became interested in dinosaurs. It was almost entirely because of my brother, Chris. He's four years younger than I am, and as a 10-year-old he was still obsessed with dinosaurs. He had more than a hundred dinosaur books in his room, lots of dinosaur toys, and dinosaur posters on his walls. He had turned his room into a little dinosaur museum. My room was more like a sports museum, with pennants and baseball cards everywhere.

There was going to be a science fair at school, and Chris wanted to do something about dinosaurs for it. He asked me to help out. I started going through books with him to gather information. And after not caring about dinosaurs *forever*, I suddenly got hooked.

A little after this, we got a computer at home for the first time. And although the Internet then was nothing like it is today, a lot of big museums had websites with information about their exhibits and the things their paleontologists were researching. You could get on mailing lists to follow all the news about discoveries. I started obsessively reading about dinosaurs and fossils. Maybe because of my earlier love of history, I wasn't interested in dinosaurs as objects or monsters. I saw them as incredible clues to how our planet had changed and evolved. That was when I knew I wanted to make paleontology my career. As for Chris, who was so into dinosaurs when we were kids, he went on to study history!

A lot of the paleontologists I know are really interested in history. Fossils are sort of like manuscripts, or ancient scrolls, that give us clues to the past. The museums we work in are archives, where we try to piece together the things that happened a long time ago based on those clues, and put them together as stories that help us understand events, revolutions, and extinctions. I guess a paleontologist really is a type of historian.

As you explore this book, be on the lookout for my stories and insights as we learn more about dinosaurs together.

—Steve Brusatte

STEVE AND HIS TEAMMATES WORKING IN ROMANIA

TYRANNOSAURUS REX,
THE GREATEST DINOSAUR
SUPERSTAR OF ALL

CHAPTER 1

SUPERSTARS
OF THE
MESOZOIC ERA

INTRODUCTION

I WAS A TEENAGER WHEN THE BEST-PRESERVED AND MOST COMPLETE

skeleton of a *T. rex*—Sue—went on display at the Field Museum in Chicago, Illinois, U.S.A. I grew up about 75 miles (121 km) away, in Ottawa, Illinois. There weren't many museums

STEVE BRUSATTE

where I lived, so the Field was kind of my hometown museum.

Walking into the room where Sue was on display, I remember thinking how enormous it was ... and scary. I was mesmerized, and seeing Sue confirmed that I wanted to be a paleontologist. After all, this was one of the biggest predators to ever live on land in the history of Earth. And it was a real animal! It hatched and grew up; it moved and ate; it saw and heard and breathed.

For about 10 years, tyrannosaurs have been a major focus of my work. I've described several new species of tyrannosaurs, like *Qianzhousaurus, Timurlengia, Juratyrant,* and *Alioramus altai.* I've constructed family trees to help us understand how dinosaurs evolved from their human-size ancestors into terrifying tyrants. And as it turns

out, tyrannosaurs originated more than 100 million years before *T. rex* came onto the scene. But for most of their history tyrannosaurs were humble animals, living in the shadows of other giant predators, like the allosaurs, ceratosaurs, and spinosaurs. That changed during the final 20 million years of the Age of Dinosaurs (also known as the Mesozoic era). That's when, for reasons we still don't really know, tyrannosaurs started to reach their huge size and began to dominate North America and Asia. They were enormous predators that stood alone on the top of the food chain. There were no other predators even approaching them in size at the time—and that remains true today, with polar bears as the current largest predators on land.

One of the reasons I think people find dinosaurs so fascinating is they were, in many ways, even more fantastic than the creatures we humans have created in our myths and legends: the monsters, dragons, and unicorns in old fairy tales. But dinosaurs were real. And more than any other dinosaur, *T. rex,* with its huge head, tiny arms, long balancing tail, and muscular legs, truly encapsulates everything we find amazing about dinosaurs!

CAMPTOSAURUS SURROUNDED BY THREE HUNGRY PREDATORS

IT WAS A REAL ANIMAL! IT HATCHED AND GREW UP; IT MOVED AND ATE; IT SAW AND HEARD AND BREATHED.

STEVE BRUSATTE AND HIS TEAM IN PORTUGAL

DINOSAURS RULED EARTH

and, in some ways, they still do! It's now been about 66 million years since the last of these fearfully great lizards roamed the planet.

Dinosaurs Forever!

Fans—both old and new—just can't seem to learn enough about them, and it's easy to see why. Scientists are always making new discoveries. No one can predict when a new paleontological dig will unearth the next big find.

Maybe one day we'll solve the remaining mysteries about how dinosaurs evolved and how they spent their time here on Earth. But for now, it's exciting to think about all the amazing things we've already learned about them. And we can look forward to all the thrilling discoveries to come. That's part of the reason we love dinosaurs so much!

We also love dinosaurs for this simple reason: No creature so huge has walked on land since the biggest dinosaurs died out. Some dinosaurs stood taller than modern apartment buildings, others had skulls as large as your dining table, and some had teeth as long as your hand. All these superstars really were amazing!

The Battle for the Biggest

When paleontologists dug fossil bones out of a desert in Argentina in 2014, it didn't take long for their findings to make headlines. Newspapers

TIME MACHINE TO THE MESOZOIC

Our Earth has been around for about 4.6 billion years. Lots of changes have happened on our planet in that time! And scientists chunk these changes into blocks of a few million years each. To be able to study and discuss these blocks of time, and for everyone to understand what everyone else was talking about, scientists gave them names. They came up with a three-part system of eras, periods, and epochs. The story of humans takes place entirely in the Cenozoic era, which began 65.5 million years ago and continues on to today. Our early ancestors emerged in the middle part of that era, at the end of the Neogene period.

But this book takes place earlier. All the action in it happens in the Mesozoic era, which began 251 million years ago and ended 65.5 million years ago. The Mesozoic is divided into three periods: the Triassic, the Jurassic, and the Cretaceous.

CENOZOIC ERA (65.5 MYA (MILLION YEARS AGO) TO PRESENT)

QUATERNARY PERIOD (2.6 MYA TO PRESENT)
HOLOCENE EPOCH (11,700 YA TO PRESENT)
PLEISTOCENE EPOCH (2.6 MYA TO 11,700 YA)

NEOGENE PERIOD (23.03–2.6 MYA)
HOLOCENE EPOCH (11,500 YA–PRESENT)
PLEISTOCENE EPOCH (1.8 MYA–11,500 YA)
PLIOCENE EPOCH (5.33–1.8 MYA)
MIOCENE EPOCH (23.03–5.33 MYA)

PALEOGENE PERIOD (65.5–23.03 MYA)
OLIGOCENE EPOCH (33.9–23.03 MYA)
EOCENE EPOCH (55.8–33.9 MYA)
PALEOCENE (65.5–55.8 MYA)

MESOZOIC ERA (251 TO 65.5 MYA)

CRETACEOUS PERIOD (145.5–66.5 MYA)
UPPER (100.5–65.5 MYA)
LOWER (145.5–100.5 MYA)

JURASSIC PERIOD (199.6–145.5 MYA)
UPPER (163–145.5 MYA)
MIDDLE (174–163 MYA)
LOWER (199.6–174 MYA)

TRIASSIC PERIOD (251–199.6 MYA)
UPPER (237–199.6 MYA)
MIDDLE (247–237 MYA)
LOWER (251–247 MYA)

around the world announced that the biggest dinosaur had been found! At first, scientists called this new species of sauropod the Titanosaur (before naming it *Patagotitan mayorum* in 2017) and estimated its size at 122 feet (37.2 m) long and around 170,000 pounds (77,111 kg).

This gargantuan plant-eater, or herbivore, may have been the biggest discovered to date, but it wasn't alone. Though we often imagine giant carnivores, or meat-eaters, rumbling across the earth as they sprinted after prey, when it came to sheer size, they were no match for the towering herbivores.

Huge Herbivores

The very first herbivore dinosaurs were small. But over the centuries, the herbivores grew bigger and bigger and bigger ... until the group of dinosaurs known as the titanosaurs emerged. This group of long-necked, small-headed, scaly-skinned, plant-eating sauropods existed pretty much everywhere on Earth until dinosaurs went extinct.

About 50 species of titanosaurs have been found so far. Every day, the largest of them had to eat plant matter totaling the weight of a car in order to feel full. How could there possibly be enough plants to go around? The plants titanosaurs ate depended on where they lived and the heights they could reach. These plants included palms, palm-tree-like plants called cycads, cone-bearing plants called conifers, and some grasses. Scientists think coexisting titanosaur species had specialized diets: One species may have eaten mostly leaves, and another ate mostly woodier plant material. This kind of selective feeding would have allowed them all to thrive, and for some to grow to gigantic heights.

Although we refer to them as titans, not all of them grew to enormous size. For example, *Magyarosaurus,* which lived in current-day

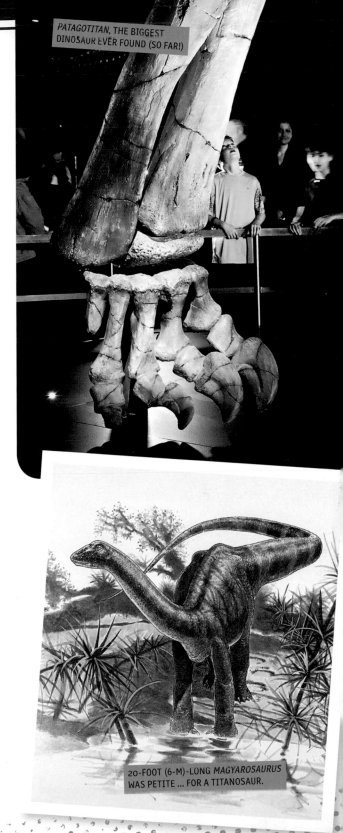

PATAGOTITAN, THE BIGGEST DINOSAUR EVER FOUND (SO FAR!)

20-FOOT (6-M)-LONG *MAGYAROSAURUS* WAS PETITE ... FOR A TITANOSAUR.

central Europe, was a mere 20 feet (6.1 m) and weighed less than a ton (907.2 kg). That makes *Magyarosaurus* as long as a giraffe and lighter than a polar bear!

Argentinosaurus really was a titan, though. For many years, it reigned as the biggest of these bigs. Pieces of a massive specimen were first discovered in Argentina, where it gets its name. Paleontologists found fossilized ribs, a few vertebrae, and a thighbone from the top of its leg. Another bone, from its lower leg, measured over five feet (1.5 m) long. That's probably at least as tall as you are!

In reconstructing *Argentinosaurus*, scientists figured it was about 115 feet (35 m) long. It carried its 120,000 pounds (54,431 kg) on four short legs. It had a heavy, flexible tail and a long, thick neck it used for grazing from the tops of trees in the forests where it lived. Its teeth, which looked like sharpened pencils, were suited for grinding and chewing all sorts of tough plant material, like the needles and cones of prehistoric conifer trees. These trees are similar to the fir and pine trees that grow in our forests today.

In 2014, *Patagotitan* took over the title of "biggest" from *Argentinosaurus*. It's so big that the head and neck of the life-size model of it go right out the door of the museum room where it lives. That's not so surprising when you consider that its thighbone alone is eight feet (2.4 m) tall. In all, 223 of this dinosaur's bones (but only one tooth and no

MASSIVE *ARGENTINOSAURUS* WAS TRULY TITANIC.

IN RECONSTRUCTING *ARGENTINOSAURUS*, SCIENTISTS FIGURED IT WAS ABOUT 115 FEET (35 M) LONG.

ARGENTINOSAURUS HUINCULENSIS

PATAGOTITAN'S THIGHBONE IS EIGHT FEET (2.4 M) TALL.

IT'S NOT EASY BEING HUGE

WHEN YOU WEIGH 85 TONS (77 t), every step you take is *heavy*. Your weight makes the earth tremble beneath you. And carrying it around puts enormous stress on your body. In fact, scientists think the largest of the dinosaurs basically maxed out their size. There's no way their skeletons could have supported any extra pounds.

So how did these massive beasts manage to do anything at all? *Patagotitan* had a number of special adaptations. For example, its long tail balanced its long neck. And it would have swayed back and forth as it walked, helping it move its back legs. It also had a strange way of standing on its four trunk-like legs, which splayed slightly outward. That stance helped the legs absorb some of *Patagotitan*'s vast weight. The titanosaur's interlocking backbones also offered support. Some of those bones were hollow, which meant they were lighter, too.

Paleontologists think *Patagotitan* may have had a large four-chambered heart—more like birds' and mammals' hearts than the three-chambered hearts found in modern-day reptiles. *Patagotitan*'s heart was six feet (1.8 m) in circumference. It weighed over 500 pounds (227 kg) and pumped 24 gallons (90.8 L) of blood through its body every five seconds. But with its heart so far from its toes, scientists wonder: How did blood from its extremities make it all the way back to its chest? They think the answer lies in the tight skin around *Patagotitan*'s ankles, which would have squeezed its ankles like the compression socks some athletes wear, giving the remote regions of its body the force to shoot blood back up into its faraway heart.

THE TAIL OF *PATAGOTITAN* BALANCED ITS NECK.

PATAGOTITAN'S HEART WAS SIX FEET (1.8 M) IN CIRCUMFERENCE.

THE SUCCESS OF THE PLANT-EATERS

APATOSAURUS ON THE HUNT FOR PLANTS

PLANT-EATING DINOSAURS FAR OUTNUMBERED their meat-eating cousins in the Jurassic and Cretaceous periods. In fact, for every big, frightening meat-eater roaming Earth, there were a hundred plant-eaters. This means not only that there must have been plenty of plants for them to eat but also that dinosaurs were especially good at eating all the different types of plants that evolved on our planet. And not just the leaves of the plants but also bark, roots, pinecones, stems, branches—you name it. How were they able to do this? By developing highly specialized teeth (see chapter 3). Teeth let the sauropods rule the planet!

skull) were dug up from a site in Argentina. This makes *Patagotitan* one of the most complete dinosaur skeletons ever discovered.

But was it truly the most titanic dinosaur of all? Some scientists don't think so. They've placed their bets on *Amphicoelias.* Don't worry if you've never heard of it. *Amphicoelias* is one of the great mysteries in dinosaur paleontology. Back in the 1870s, an enormous femur and a five-foot (1.5-m) vertebra were dug up out of the rocky ground in central Colorado, U.S.A. The paleontologist who found these fossil bones took notes and sketched them. He estimated that the dinosaur they belonged to was 190 feet (57.9 m) long and 220,000 pounds (99,790 kg)! He then packed the bones up and sent them off by train to the American Museum of Natural History in New York.

Did those bones ever arrive at their destination? We have no idea, because they have been missing ever since. And no one has a clue about what might have become of them. Lots of paleontologists have shown up at the museum over the years to look for them in the fossil collection. But so far, no one has had any luck. Will those bones ever turn up to prove that *Amphicoelias* was bigger than *Patagotitan*? Or will the discovery of a new megaspecies one day unseat *Patagotitan*?

Colossal Carnivores

No doubt about it, *Tyrannosaurus rex,* which lived 66–67 million years ago, was a big, fearsome dinosaur. The meaning of its name, "tyrant lizard king," says it all. It was the original King of Beasts—long before the first lion was ever born.

When a reconstructed *T. rex* skeleton was exhibited at the American Museum of Natural History in New York City in 1906, scientists thought they had found the biggest meat-eater that had ever lived.

So exactly how big are we talking here? The biggest *T. rex* discovered so far was dug up in South Dakota, U.S.A., in the 1980s. That *T. rex* is Sue. She is really impressive for a few reasons. For starters, she's the most complete *T. rex* skeleton ever found, with 90 percent of her remains unearthed by a fossil hunter named Sue Hendrickson. Sue the *T. rex* measures 42 feet (12.8 m) from end to end, and is 13 feet (4 m) tall. Her skull alone weighs 600 pounds (272 kg). That plus her muscles, organs, and the rest of her all put together probably weighed about 18,000 pounds (8,165 kg) when she was still alive.

Like the other biggest of the big predators, Sue was a theropod (we'll explain what this means in chapter 2). She and the other *T. rexes* evolved into existence near the end of the dinosaurs' time on Earth, in the Cretaceous period. The carnivores that came before her weren't anywhere near as big. Scientists think Sue's species evolved to its massive size only after it grew a large enough brain to help it outsmart its prey—and eat more of them.

SUE IS THE MOST COMPLETE *T. REX* SKELETON EVER FOUND.

THE BETTER TO EAT YOU WITH: SUE'S TEETH

MY, WHAT TINY ARMS YOU HAVE

ONE OF THE GREAT MYSTERIES OF PALEONTOLOGY has always been what *T. rex*'s arms were used for—and why they were so shrimpy. They were so incredibly muscular and powerful that each arm could lift more than 400 pounds (181 kg)! So it stands to reason that those stumpy little limbs served an important purpose. But what was it? Some scientists think they evolved this way to offset all that extra weight in *T. rex* 's head. In truth, though, scientists have lots of theories but haven't been able to prove any.

WHY WERE *T. REX*'S ARMS SO SMALL?

T. REX SCAVENGING A MEAL FROM AN ALREADY-DEAD *TRICERATOPS*

It would have been terrifying to run into Sue out there among the trees. Her green-tinged knobby scales would have helped her blend in with her surroundings—until she was ready for a snack! Imagine her springing out at you with huge jaws filled with about 60 ser-rated teeth as big as bananas. One of Sue's recovered teeth measures 12 inches (30.5 cm) long. Those teeth could crunch through bones—your bones (if you'd been alive 67 million years ago), *Triceratops*'s bones, even the bones of other *T. rexes*. Because, yes, Sue was a cannibal.

She could sniff you out with her terrific sense of smell. In fact, her olfactory bulb (the part of the brain that senses smell) was about the size of a golf ball. And that was pretty big compared to the olfactory bulbs of other dinosaurs. Sue could chase you down on her two nimble back legs. Each of her tiny arms ended in two sharp claws.

A *T. REX*'S TEETH WERE AS BIG AS BANANAS.

GIGANOTOSAURUS HAD BIG, STABBY TEETH, AND SHARP CLAWS AT THE ENDS OF ITS STUBBY ARMS.

Some scientists speculate that Sue was a scavenger instead of a predator, feeding on already-dead animals. She may actually have been both.

No one knows for sure if Sue was really a female. But some scientists have proposed the idea that female *T. rexes* were heftier than their male counterparts. Up to 1,000 pounds (454 kg) heavier, in fact.

T. rex wasn't the only big meat-eater around, though. In 1995, the world learned about what was possibly the second-biggest carnivore. That's the year two paleontologists described a new species of meat-eater they found in Argentina. They called it *Giganotosaurus.* It lived about 30 million years before *T. rex* in swampy parts of the southern hemisphere. It grew to be about the same length as *T. rex* but weighed only 12,000 pounds (5,443 kg). But still, yikes!

Like *T. rex, Giganotosaurus* had big, stabby teeth, and sharp claws at the ends of its stubby arms—three claws, though, instead of *T. rex's* two. It's possible it hunted in packs, using those claws to slash at some unlucky titanosaur before crushing it with its powerful jaws. Its teeth were

like those you might find inside the mouth of a shark. It used them for chomping on the legs of its prey, to weaken it and bring it down.

To date, very few *Giganotosaurus* fossils have been found. Scientists have less information about it than they do about *T. rex.* This makes it hard for them to figure out how this monster achieved its monstrous size. Maybe it started maturing at a really young age. Maybe it lived for a long time, so it had many years to grow extra huge. We might not find the answer unless we find more *Giganotosaurus* fossils.

Scientists did find a new, huge megapredator back in 2014, though. It's longer—and weirder—than its predecessors. Named *Spinosaurus,* which means "thorn lizard," it may have become famous only recently, but it was first found around 1911 in Egypt's Sahara desert. The paleontologist who excavated its bones took them to Munich, Germany, to study. But during World War II, Munich was bombed and all the *Spinosaurus* fossils were destroyed. Evidence of *Spinosaurus's* awesomeness went up in flames.

SPINOSAURUS HAD A SAIL ON ITS BACK—NOT UNLIKE THE ONE ON THIS SAILFISH.

Fast-forward a few decades, and *Spinosaurus* was rediscovered in a different part of the Sahara. The new specimen was located in Morocco, which is 2,340 miles (3,766 km) and three countries away from Egypt. This time around, scientists managed to give it a good, long study. Using the bones they'd found and also 3-D imaging technology, they determined that it may have been about 55 feet (16.8 m) long—which could mean it was longer than Sue the *T. rex*. For all its length, *Spinosaurus* was on the skinny side, weighing in at around 16,000 pounds (7,257 kg). *Spinosaurus* had a sail, which was supported by six-foot (1.8-m)-long bones, on its back. Some scientists think the sail helped keep it cool by radiating excess body heat. Or it may have kept it warm by soaking up sunrays. Other scientists think the sail was filled with fat, which allowed *Spinosaurus* to store food and water—like the humps on a camel.

DESCRIBING FOSSILS

STEVE BRUSATTE

WHEN PALEONTOLOGISTS TALK ABOUT describing a fossil, we're describing the way we study them, then publish what we've learned. We compare the fossil to lots of other dinosaurs, then write up a description of its bones, take photographs and make drawings of the bones, put the dinosaur into a family tree, and then determine whether it is a new species (and if so, we get to name it!). Then we put all of this together into a report (a scientific paper) that we send to a journal (a type of magazine that's read by other scientists). The report is sent out for peer review, where other scientists read it, critique it, make suggestions, and decide whether the evidence is strong enough to be published. If they say yes, our report is published and we have described a new dinosaur. If they say no, we have to do some more work and make our report better.

WE COMPARE THE FOSSIL TO LOTS OF OTHER DINOSAURS AND THEN WRITE UP A DESCRIPTION OF ITS BONES.

GIGANOTOSAURUS

REGALICERATOPS APPEARED TO BE A COMBINATION OF A CHAMOSAURINE AND A CENTROSAURINE.

Spinosaurus also had a huge skull and large, snapping crocodile-like jaws used for eating fish. Oddly, it seems *Spinosaurus* was not just a land dinosaur. It was semiaquatic. It could dive right into rivers and swim around to hunt for a feast of coelacanths and spiny sharks. A few specialized features helped it do this:

1. Nostrils on the top of its snout that allowed *Spinosaurus* to breathe when part of its head was underwater
2. A unique body shape that was better suited to paddling around than walking
3. Birdlike feet that may actually have been webbed

Big and weird—what else could you ask for in a dinosaur?

CHECK OUT *SPINOSAURUS*'S SNAPPING CROCODILE JAWS!

FUNNY FEATURES

SPINOSAURUS'S SAIL MAKES IT stand out among dinosaurs. But it's not the only one with an odd feature that's puzzled scientists. Paleontologists also study the features of the ceratopsians. These dinosaurs are characterized by the different horns, frills, and knobs decorating their heads. Chamosaurines are dinosaurs with small horns over their noses, big horns over their eyes, and long frills around their necks. Centrosaurines have big horns over their noses, small horns over their eyes, and short frills.

In 2005, paleontologists dug up a new ceratopsian in Canada. It wasn't quite a chamosaurine or a centrosaurine. It was a little of both, with a long nose horn, tiny horns over its eyes, and a massive frill. It's named *Regaliceratops*, and it got scientists thinking about how ceratopsians evolved—and why. Just as paleontologists will go on trying to figure out the differences among ceratopsians, they'll also keep trying to understand what *Spinosaurus* used its sail for.

OTHER MAJOR BIGS

DINOSAURS CAME IN MANY SHAPES AND SIZES. And they didn't have to be titanosaurs or massive meat-eaters to achieve superstar status. Check out these other major bigs.

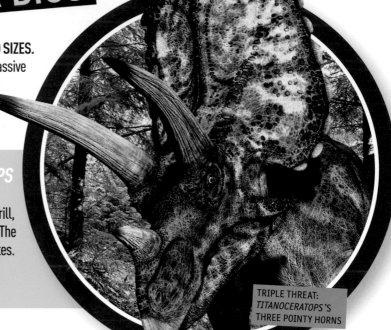

BIGGEST SKULL: *TITANOCERATOPS*

LIVED: Late Cretaceous
FEATURES: Three massive horns and a head frill, which may have protected it from predators. The frill also might have been used to attract mates. All told, the skull measured an incredible 10.5 feet (3.2 m) tall.

TRIPLE THREAT: *TITANOCERATOPS*'S THREE POINTY HORNS

BIGGEST DUCKBILL: *SHANTUNGOSAURUS* OR *MAGNAPAULIA*

LIVED: Late Cretaceous
FEATURES: Both of these duck-billed herbivores were about 50 feet (15.2 m) long. *Shantungosaurus,* from China, weighed around 32,000 pounds (14,515 kg). It turned everything it ate into fine pulp with its 1,000 powerful teeth. *Magnapaulia* may have weighed as much as 50,000 pounds (22,680 kg) and may have been able to swim.

SHANTUNGOSAURUS GROUND ITS FOOD WITH ITS 1,000 TEETH.

FEATHERS—NOT FOR FLIGHT—FOR 2,000-POUND (907-KG) *UTAHRAPTOR*

BIGGEST RAPTOR: *UTAHRAPTOR*

LIVED: Early Cretaceous
FEATURES: Walked on two clawed feet and had feathered arms that ended in long, thick talons that could slash or stab. Measured 20 feet (6.1 m) long and weighed 2,000 pounds (907 kg). Dined on meat.

LONGEST DINOSAUR: *DIPLODOCUS*

LIVED: Late Jurassic
FEATURES: Herbivorous sauropod that grew to be 108 feet (32.9 m) and had a 46-foot (14-m) tail!

THE TALLEST OF THEM ALL: *SAUROPOSEIDON*

DIPLODOCUS MAY HAVE SNAPPED ITS TAIL AT PREDATORS.

TALLEST DINOSAUR: *SAUROPOSEIDON*

LIVED: Early Cretaceous
FEATURES: Sauropod that grew to 110 feet (33.5 m) and could reach branches 55 feet (16.8 m) up.

LONG NECK AND TINY BRAIN FOR *MAMENCHISAURUS*

LONGEST NECK: *MAMENCHISAURUS*

LIVED: Late Jurassic
FEATURES: Plant-eating sauropod with a 50-foot (15.2-m) neck.

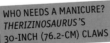

WHO NEEDS A MANICURE? *THERIZINOSAURUS*'S 30-INCH (76.2-CM) CLAWS

LONGEST CLAWS: *THERIZINOSAURUS*

LIVED: Late Cretaceous
FEATURES: Omnivorous theropod (it ate both plants and animals) that may have grown to 33 feet (10.1 m) long and had wings and feathers. *Therizinosaurus* walked around on two feet that had four claws each. Claws on the ends of its wing-arms were 30 inches (76.2 cm) long—those claws were about as long as an adult's footstep.

AMAZING WINGS

THE *ZHENYUANLONG SUNI* FOSSIL WAS FOUND by a farmer in northeastern China, who sold it to a museum. That's how I got involved working with it, studying it, and finally, describing it. It is a feathered cousin of *Velociraptor* from about 125 million years ago, in the early Cretaceous period. It's the biggest winged dinosaur, at least that we have good records of. This is one of the many feathered dinosaurs that have been found in China, and it comes from the same general place as those others, Liaoning, which is in the northeastern part of the country.

Zhenyuanlong would have looked a lot like *Velociraptor,* but slightly bigger—about the size of a goat. It had sharp teeth, big claws on its feet, and of course, it was covered in feathers. It had proper wings, but its arms were a lot shorter than *Velociraptor*'s and those of most modern birds. So it didn't have big enough arms to fly and probably didn't have big enough muscles in its chest, either. It evolved its wings from its ancestors, and there are two possible reasons for this evolution. One is that *Zhenyuanlong*'s wings let it do other things—maybe it used them for display purposes or to keep its eggs warm. It's also possible that *Zhenyuanlong*'s ancestors were able to fly, then got bigger and bigger until they lost the ability to fly and became more like ostriches.

My colleague Junchang Lü, a Chinese paleontologist, saw the first photos of the fossil. What is so neat about it are its really big, beautiful wings. He got excited and showed the photos to me, and then I got excited and went out to China to look at it with him. It's in a big slab of limestone, and the bones really stick out. They're a lot darker in color than the rock around them, which is dull

STEVE BRUSATTE

WHAT *ZHENYUANLONG* MAY HAVE LOOKED LIKE

THIS ZHENYUANLONG FOSSIL IS IN A BIG SLAB OF LIMESTONE, AND THE BONES REALLY STICK OUT.

STEVE AND JUNCHANG LÜ WITH THE *ZHENYUANLONG SUNI* FOSSIL

and gray. Most of the skeleton is there, and it looks like something out of an art museum. It's one of the most beautiful fossils I've ever seen, and it's so remarkable that it has feather impressions, which we were able to study in addition to its bones. We cataloged its anatomy by comparing it to other dinosaurs, and that's how we were able to put it on the *Velociraptor* family tree.

In a case like this, where I'm called in to study a fossil that's already been found by someone else, there is a process I follow. I try to gather as much information as possible before I go and look at photos to get an idea of what the specimen is. Then I'm eventually set loose with the specimen and tasked with making sense of it. We do lots of comparisons with other dinosaurs, and for that we really rely on our own experience. It's like how a doctor treats a patient who comes in complaining about symptoms. He or she knows that certain diseases usually have certain symptoms, and can identify

the disease by asking the patient about his or her symptoms. Paleontologists know that different dinosaurs have different types of skeletons—differences in the size and shapes of their bones, or the presence or absence of horns, spikes, or long necks—and we can identify a dinosaur based on what type of skeleton it has.

We learn a lot about anatomy in school, and we put that knowledge to use, plus we take measurements, make drawings, and record whether they have or do not have certain features. This all goes into a spreadsheet. We then use a computer to turn that spreadsheet into a family tree, grouping dinosaurs as close relatives if they share a lot of features. It's something that takes a lot of time, because it's so meticulous, like working at a crime scene!

What's So Great About Being Big?

It's hard to imagine what the advantages of growing as big as *Argentinosaurus* might have been. After all, the bigger the dinosaur, the more resources it needed in order to live. So why would it be beneficial for any creature to grow to such an enormous size? And why did some species of dinosaurs continually evolve into even bigger dinosaurs? Scientists don't know all the answers for certain, but they do have some ideas.

First, having a big, bulky body as an herbivore could be a great defense against sharp-toothed, hungry predators like *T. rex*. Even for a seasoned hunter that's armed with powerful jaws and brutal claws, it's not so easy to take down an animal that's the size of an apartment building. To go along with their girth, some sauropods had thick, scaly skin that would have been difficult to bite through—another useful defense against all the animals that wanted to eat them.

The biggest of the titanosaurs may also have grown so big in order to get to resources other animals couldn't reach—like the tops of trees. While everyone else was scrounging along the ground or in the rivers for tasty edibles, the biggest of the herbivores could go high. That way,

REACHING HIGH BRANCHES WAS A BREEZE FOR BRACHIOSAURUS.

DID MEGADINOSAURS, LIKE DIAMANTINASAURUS, HAVE HOLLOW BONES?

there was enough food to go around, and for a lot of different species.

As for *how* those megadinosaurs managed to grow so big, well, scientists have theories about that, too. Part of it may have had to do with the fact that some dinosaurs had hollow bones. That meant they were lightweight, so their frames could support more bulk. Another theory is that those sauropods didn't bother chewing the plant matter they dined on. They just ripped off bark and branches and swallowed them whole. Their big bodies featured bigger, longer digestive tracts for breaking down all that woody, pulpy plant matter. And by the time dinner made its way to the, um, end of the line—days or even weeks later—the dinosaur had gotten every last bit of nutrition out of its meal. Perhaps all those extra vitamins helped them grow to extraordinary sizes.

Another theory suggests a connection between the biggest of the carnivorous dinosaurs and the shape of their heads. Recently, scientists studying the strange bumps and frills on meat-eating theropods' heads made an interesting discovery. The theropods that evolved to be the biggest also had intricate ornaments growing out of their craniums. In fact, 20 out of the 22 biggest theropods had some kind of fancy headgear. What's the precise connection between those decorations and all that dinosaur bulk? Scientists are still trying to work all that out. But some think that these embellished skulls may have helped the flashiest theropods find mates, claim their territory, or defend themselves. Those would have been some pretty big advantages!

GOING SMALL

SOME MAJORLY MASSIVE LAND ANIMALS roamed prehistoric Earth. But what about the other end of the spectrum—the absolute smallest of the small? Creatures in this category don't disappoint, either. Dinosaurs the size of a gecko must have had a very different life from Sue and her companions!

A DINO THE SIZE OF A SHOEBOX

MICRORAPTOR

LIVED: Early Cretaceous
FEATURES: Measured about 16 inches (40.6 cm) long when fully grown. It had a long, fanned tail and flight feathers on two sets of wings. Some scientists believe it may have been able to fly. *Microraptor* also had sharp little teeth likely used for munching on smaller animals and insects.

COMPSOGNATHUS WOULD HAVE SNACKED ON LIZARDS.

COMPSOGNATHUS

LIVED: Late Jurassic
FEATURES: Grew to about two feet (0.6 m)—the size of a chicken—and used its fast little legs to catch and eat lizards, which it probably swallowed whole.

IT'S POSSIBLE DINO COUSIN *SALTOPUS* HOPPED.

SALTOPUS

LIVED: Late Triassic
FEATURES: Dinosaur cousin that was two feet (0.6 m) long and weighed about two pounds (0.9 kg). It's been compared—sizewise, anyway—to a house cat. Its name means "hopping foot." Did it actually hop? Scientists aren't sure.

WORLD-FAMOUS *IGUANODON* WAS THE SECOND DINO EVER NAMED.

39 *IGUANODON* FOSSIL SKELETONS WERE FOUND IN ONE COAL MINE IN BELGIUM IN 1878.

The World's First Famous Dinosaur: *Iguanodon*

No, *Iguanodon* was never the biggest, the smallest, or the weirdest of the dinosaurs to roam the planet. But it was one of the first dinosaurs to ever become famous. That's because it was the first dinosaur in relatively modern times to ever be found. And, after *Megalosaurus,* it was the second dinosaur ever to be named. It's largely thanks to *Iguanodon* that people became dinosaur crazy to begin with.

When a few of *Iguanodon*'s teeth were picked out of a quarry in the south of England in 1822, the word "dinosaur" hadn't even been made up yet. Sure, people had found all sorts of dinosaur fossils for thousands of years. But they had absolutely no idea what they were. In 1822, Charles Darwin had not yet published his theories about evolution. No one knew that different kinds of animals had come and gone over the

IGUANODON COULD NIP FOOD WITH ITS BEAK.

millennia. To these researchers, the discovery of *Iguanodon*'s big teeth and, later, its big bones, meant that huge lizards were still wandering around somewhere. Needless to say, many found this a frightening possibility.

Little by little, pioneering paleontologists began to understand that *Iguanodon* was not actually a giant iguana (its name means "iguana tooth"). They also figured out that no *Iguanodons* were left alive anywhere on Earth. These revelations fueled what was to become a craze for dinosaur bones. For some dedicated fossil hunters and scientists, that craze is still going on, as strong and as important as ever.

Iguanodon has been studied since the early 19th century, and lots of *Iguanodon* bones have been found since then. That means scientists have been studying it for longer than almost any other kind of dinosaur. So they know quite a lot about it. It lived about 125 million years ago—all over Europe. It was about the height—but more than twice the

TRACKS ARE CLUES TO DINO SIZE, WEIGHT, AND MORE!

weight—of an African elephant, growing to a length of almost 30 feet (9.1 m) and weighing 30,000 pounds (13,608 kg). The scaly-skinned ornithopod ate plants, which it grasped in its five-fingered hands. And it nibbled at its food with sharp teeth that lined the inside of its beak.

Back in the 19th century, scientists thought that *Iguanodon* walked on all fours. But after years of study, they shifted to a new theory that *Iguanodon* walked upright on two feet, with its tail dragging along the ground to give it balance. That thinking recently changed again. They now believe that *Iguanodon* sometimes walked on four limbs, and sometimes on two. It would have been fastest on two limbs, so maybe it stood on its feet when it had to run away from something. It's also possible that *Iguanodon* moved around on two limbs as a baby, and became more comfortable on four limbs as it got older. It had a big spike on its thumb, which it may have used to defend itself against predators. Like other plant-eaters, it very likely lived in herds.

What more is there to learn about *Iguanodon*? Probably a lot! Even today, scientists continue to study this fascinating first.

MEASURING UP

IT'S RARE FOR FOSSIL HUNTERS to find complete dinosaur skeletons. So how do scientists figure out important information from a handful of bones, like how big and heavy dinosaurs were? They have a lot of tricks up their sleeves. First, they might compare the dinosaur in question to what they know about the size and weight of living animals, like elephants. They might also compare the bones of a dinosaur species to the bones of a related species and use those to make their estimates. They can also study fossilized dinosaur tracks. These are common but still exciting finds. The tracks provide clues to how heavily dinosaurs stepped, and that helps suggest their weight and also how fast they could walk or run.

These days, scientists use computer models to help them gauge what dinosaurs might have looked like and how they moved. Recently, scientists in England used computer models to understand how the sauropods evolved into such huge creatures, and what the distinct shapes of their bodies might have had to do with it. They found that the earliest sauropods balanced their weight in their hips, so they could walk on two feet. But as sauropods got bigger, they became front heavy and started walking on four feet. Scientists think that this shift in weight is what helped the titanosaurs, especially, grow to such enormous sizes and, unlike smaller sauropods, to survive all the way to the end of the time of the dinosaurs 66 million years ago.

DIG IN

ARE YOU A PALEO PRO? Identify each of these prehistoric superstars from the clues!

1. This creature has crocodile-like jaws, possibly for eating fish.

2. This decadent dino has a long nose horn, horns over the eyes, and a massive head frill.

3. With an eight-foot (2.4-m) femur and a heart that's six feet (1.8 m) in circumference, this is one colossal creature.

B PATAGOTITAN MAYORUM

4. This 16-inch (40.6-cm) dino had an additional set of flight gear.

5. This winged dino was the size of a goat.

6. This massive meat-eater has a skull weighing 600 pounds (272 kg).

A T. REX

C SPINOSAURUS

D REGALICERATOPS

E MICRORAPTOR

F ZHENYUANLONG SUNI

ANSWER KEY: 1. c; 2. d; 3. b; 4. e; 5. f; 6. a

CHAPTER 2

HERE COME THE DINOSAURS

PREHISTORIC "SNAPSHOT" OF DINOSAURS AND FLYING REPTILES

LAYER AFTER LAYER OF FOOTPRINTS AND TRACKS,

and each layer of rock, with all its different kinds of footprints, was like another page in a book.

STEVE BRUSATTE

At first, we didn't know what they were—only that the tracks were amazing.

My colleagues in central Poland had discovered the tracks which had been left behind by the ancestors of dinosaurs. By studying them, we could tell how these different kinds of animals changed over time—if they got bigger or smaller over the centuries, if they died out and other new species appeared to take their place. We thought maybe these were all reptile tracks.

I went out to that part of Poland to do fieldwork, and with my friend Grzegorz Niedźwiedzki, a young paleontologist from Poland, I found even more of these prints and trackways.

It can be difficult to find an animal's fossilized skeleton, since each animal has only one skeleton. But one animal can leave millions of footprints behind, if it lives in an environment where they can be preserved. So it's much easier for a

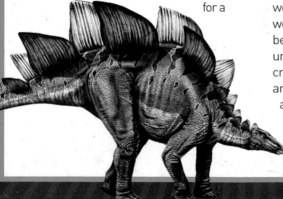

paleontologist to find trackways, and from these trackways we're able to learn a lot about the animals that made them. And after studying these, we learned that they were made by the precursors of dinosaurs—their closest relatives, which were living in the earliest part of the Triassic period. The tracks are from a creature called *Prorotodactylus*. These kinds of tracks are quite rare, and the ones we found in Poland gave us a glimpse of where dinosaurs came from.

The tracks were small, only about a couple of centimeters, and there were both footprints and handprints, so these creatures were walking on all fours. From the size of the prints and their spacing, we could tell how big the animals were, which was roughly the size of a house cat. More than that, these prints helped us realize that the direct ancestors of dinosaurs emerged much earlier than we had originally thought. It was not the story I was expecting!

We also learned something else we weren't expecting: The massive dinosaurs we know about today had a humble beginning. They started out as meek, unassuming, awkward, long-limbed creatures living in the shadow of other animals, such as reptiles, amphibians, and early mammals. You'd never think that these creatures would produce descendants that evolved into *T. rex* and *Brontosaurus*!

TRACKWAYS OF DINOSAUR ANCESTORS FOUND IN POLAND

IT CAN BE **DIFFICULT** TO FIND AN ANIMAL'S **FOSSILIZED SKELETON,** SINCE EACH ANIMAL HAS ONLY ONE SKELETON.

PROROTODACTYLUS WAS ROUGHLY THE SIZE OF A HOUSE CAT.

DINOSAURS LIVED ON EARTH FOR AN ASTONISHING 165 MILLION YEARS.

But they weren't the first creatures to evolve on our planet.

There were more than 300 million years between the appearances of the first animals and the first dinosaurs. But all that time, and all those animals, had a lot to do with the dinosaurs we know and love. The time that comes right before the dinosaurs is called the Permian period.

You wouldn't have recognized our planet during those 45 million years. For starters, it had only one huge continent on it, called Pangaea. That means "all earth." The only ocean was Panthalassa, which means "all ocean." And Tethys was the only sea. It is named for one of the Titans of Greek mythology, who was the mother of river gods. Coral reefs and sponges filled these waters, and so did brachiopods—marine animals that are similar to today's organisms with hinged shells, like clams and mussels—bony fish, rays, and sharks. Some of those sharks had sharp spikes sticking out of their heads.

In the northernmost part of the planet, the weather was super hot, and it went back and forth between dry and wet. Probably the harshest environment to live in was at the center of Pangaea, far from the coasts. By the time of the Permian period, much of this area had turned from swamp to desert, so it hardly rained there at all.

Over time, Earth got drier, and plants and animals evolved to adapt to these new conditions. Once a lot of mosses had thrived. But since these plants required damp, humid conditions to grow, many of them died out during this time. Gymnosperms, plants that reproduce with seeds, mostly replaced them. In the Permian, these included conifers (like evergreens with

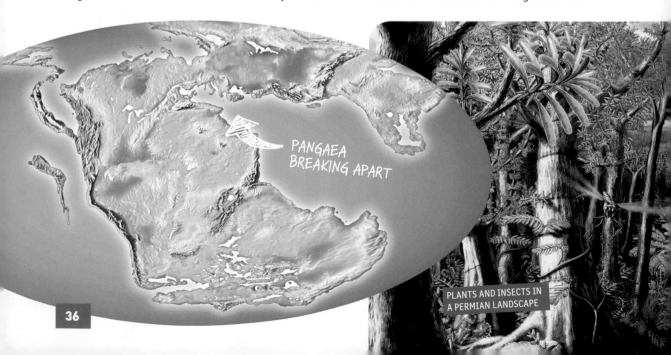

PANGAEA BREAKING APART

PLANTS AND INSECTS IN A PERMIAN LANDSCAPE

pinecones) and cycads (like today's palm trees). They also included ginkgoes and gnetophytes, some of which were scraggly shrubs or vines.

In the Permian, all kinds of insects started emerging to take advantage of the new plant species now growing on Earth—like beetles. These insects pushed out the species that came before them, like four-inch (10.2-cm)-long flying cockroaches, two-foot (0.6-m)-long dragonflies, and 6.6-foot (2-m)-long millipedes that were bigger than your dog.

Also crawling around the surface of Pangaea were reptiles such as *Dimetrodon*. This might be the most recognizable animal of the Permian period. It looked like a 500-pound (227-kg) lizard with a tall, bony sail on its back. Scientists used to think *Dimetrodon* ate plants. But when they found fossils from 39 *Dimetrodon* in Texas, U.S.A.—along with fossils of some of the things they'd eaten—scientists learned that *Dimetrodon* ate sharks and one-foot

FOSSILIZED FERNS FROM THE PERMIAN PERIOD

(0.3-m)-long amphibians called *Diplocaulus* along with other land-based animals.

Some of the Permian's reptiles were plant-eaters, such as cowlike *Moschops*. It lived in herds in the part of Pangaea that eventually broke off into what is now Africa. The first big plant-eaters lived then, too—way, *way* before the titanosaurs or even any dinosaurs emerged. They were called pareiasaurs and have been described as having barrel-shaped bodies covered with bony knobs. They also had short legs and itty-bitty skulls. Pareiasaurs weighed as much as 1,300 pounds (590 kg) and

REPTILES LIKE *DIMETRODON* PREDATED DINOSAURS.

TIMELINE

TIME ON EARTH IS DESCRIBED in terms of eras. These are the three most recent:

- **PALEOZOIC ERA: 542 MYA**

  Periods in this era include the Permian, among others:
  Permian period: 299–251 MYA
- **MESOZOIC ERA: 251 MYA**

  Periods in the Mesozoic include:
  Triassic period: 251–199.6 MYA
  Jurassic period: 199.6–145.5 MYA
  Cretaceous period: 145.5–65.5 MYA
- **CENOZOIC ERA: 65.5 MYA**

  Periods in the Cenozoic include:
  Quaternary Period: 2.6 MYA to present
  Neogene period: 23.03–2.6 MYA
  Paleogene period: 65.5–23.03 MYA

PAREIASAURS LIVED NEAR AND SWAM IN THE WATERS OF THE PERMIAN PERIOD.

hung out in damp lowland areas, spending time in bodies of water. But there still weren't any mammals on our planet, just a diverse bunch of therapsids, which are what mammals evolved from. They may have had whiskers and fur, and even been warm-blooded.

By the end of the Permian period, our planet was teeming with all sorts of life. And then, over a period of tens of thousands of years, almost every single species on Earth was wiped out.

This was the biggest extinction *ever*. More than 90 percent of all living things—plants, insects, animals, marine life—disappeared in a single event that some people call the Great Dying. It's also known as the Permian–Triassic extinction. It came about due to volcanic eruptions taking place in what's now Siberia.

If all this sounds tragic, consider this: Without the Permian–Triassic extinction, dinosaurs may never have existed. Our planet now had the space and other resources to let

dinosaurs emerge and thrive. And millions of years later, allowed humans to learn all about them—through science.

What Is a Dinosaur, Anyway?

These days, we know that what makes a dinosaur a dinosaur is a very specific set of qualities. But it wasn't always this way. When fossil-hunting expeditions started in the early 1800s, many beliefs about dinosaurs were just plain wrong. For example, even the most up-to-date scientists thought the bones they dug up belonged to giant lizards. In fact, the word "dinosaur," which was coined in 1842, means "terrible lizard." Although dinosaurs and lizards are both reptiles, they are only distantly related.

For a time scientists believed that *any* really old fossils must belong to dinosaurs, even as dinosaurs were more closely studied. These included ichthyosaurs, mosasaurs, and plesiosaurs—nondinosaurs that lived in the pre-historic ocean—and pterosaurs, which also weren't dinosaurs and flew through the skies.

Today, science has helped to make sense of all the amazing discoveries paleontologists have been making for the last 200 years. For starters, we now know that dinosaurs are vertebrates. This means they have backbones and skeletons on the insides of their bodies. Mammals like humans and horses, amphibians like frogs and salamanders, and fish are vertebrates.

In addition to being vertebrates, dinosaurs are also reptiles. Other members of this group are turtles, lizards, snakes, and crocodiles. Incredible as it might sound, birds are reptiles, too. Hard to believe? It won't be when you understand what makes an animal a reptile.

First, a reptile has scales somewhere on its body. You probably know where to find scales on a fish or a snake. (You can find scales on birds on their toes and sometimes farther up their feet and legs.) Additionally, reptiles usually lay hard-shelled eggs (although some reptiles, like some snakes, give birth to live babies). They breathe with lungs. And most reptiles are ectothermic, or cold-blooded.

Another thing that makes a dinosaur a dinosaur is that it belongs to a group of reptiles called archosaurs. Archosaurs, or ruling reptiles, evolved around the time of the Permian–Triassic extinction. A few of them survived. Since there weren't that many animals on Earth after the Great Dying, there wasn't much competition for resources like food and water and habitat. This helped the archosaurs multiply and diversify. At some point, the archosaurs split into two groups. One group went on to evolve into ancestors of crocodiles. The other group evolved into pterosaurs and dinosaurs—this group included birds. Soon, dinosaurs would begin their very slow climb to the top of the animal kingdom.

ORNITHISCHIANS VS. SAURISCHIANS

ONE OF THE MAIN BRANCHES, or "clades," of the dinosaur family is the ornithischians. Its members were the so-called bird-hipped dinosaurs. The forward-most bone in their hips—the pubis—pointed backward. The family tree on the next page describes the three major groups of ornithischian dinos.

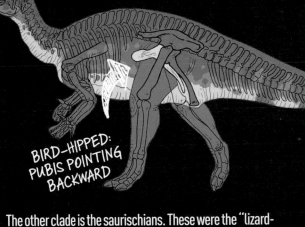

BIRD-HIPPED: PUBIS POINTING BACKWARD

The other clade is the saurischians. These were the "lizard-hipped" dinosaurs. A saurischian had a pubis that pointed down and forward. You'll see in the family tree that there are two major groups of saurischian dinosaurs. Confusingly, birds are descended from the "lizard-hipped" branch of dinosaurs!

LIZARD-HIPPED: PUBIS POINTING DOWN AND FORWARD

DINOSAUR FAMILY TREE

STEVE BRUSATTE

ARCHOSAURS

CROCODILIANS

 PTEROSAURS

DINOSAURS

ORNITHISCHIANS

SAURISCHIANS

THYREOPHORANS

STEGOSAURS   ANKYLOSAURS

PROSAUROPODS & SAUROPODS

MARGINOCEPHALIANS

CERATOPSIANS   PACHYCEPHALOSAURS

THEROPODS

TYRANNOSAURS   ORNITHOMIMIDS

ORNITHOPODS

IGUANODONTIANS   HADROSAURIANS

THERIZINOSAURS   DROMAEOSAURS   BIRDS

A BIG PART OF THE WORK I DO is build family trees for dinosaurs and other ancient animals. As with human families, these trees are useful for understanding how dino families changed during history.

When we build our own family trees, we trawl through photos, letters, and documents for information.

We can't do that with dinosaurs, of course, but we *can* use bones and teeth. As we study dinosaur fossils, we make lists of their features: Some teeth are sharp, and others are leaf-shaped. Some backbones have 10 bones in the neck area, and others have 11 or 12. Some arm bones are long, and others are short. There are plenty of clues in bones!

A LONG-NECKED PLESIOSAUR

FOSSILIZED LEAVES OF A PLANT THAT LIVED AS EARLY AS THE PERMIAN PERIOD

How Dinosaurs Evolved

So here we are, 230 million years ago. It's the middle of the Triassic period, one of the three periods that make up the Mesozoic era. Very slowly, the planet has been recovering from the devastating Permian–Triassic extinction. The land called Pangaea is still one great big blob with a desert in its center. During its hottest and driest times, wildfires break out and make it even harder for any life to exist. Most life exists at the edges of the vast continent, where the conditions are the most favorable.

But things are changing. The climate is mostly hot and dry, with rains coming in monsoon-like spurts. There's enough rain to keep certain plants and trees that survived the Great Dying alive, like gink-goes, conifers, horsetails, ferns, and enormous redwoods.

PLACODUS CRUNCHING UP SHELLFISH

Turtles, including some with teeth, live in the ocean. So do some much weirder animals, such as *Askeptosaurus,* a snake-shaped reptile with four limbs, as well as *Placodus,* a shellfish-crunching, spiny-backed reptile. There's also the totally terrifying *Nothosaurus,* which grows to about 11 feet (3.4 m) and hunts the waters for fish and squid, which it catches in its sharp teeth. It also scrambles onto shore using the five thick claws on each of its four feet. There are

ichthyosaurs in the water, too, like the *Chaohusaurus*—a six-foot (1.8-m) eely thing that gives birth to live babies right there in the water.

Toward the end of the Triassic, the oceans became home to another reptilian paddler. The first proof that these creatures emerged during this period comes from a five-foot (1.5-m) plesio-saur found in 2015 in Germany. The most impressive of the plesiosaurs wasn't the long-necked *Elasmosaurus* (although that would be a good guess, paleo pros!). It was *Albertonectes,* which was 36 feet (11 m) long, with the longest neck of any plesiosaur, measuring an incredible 23 feet (7 m)! Some reptiles glided through the sky. *Kuehneosaurus,* for example, was a small critter that made its way from tree to tree by spreading its wings and catching a draft under its armpits. And the first pterosaurs flew alongside the ocean and scooped up fish in their toothy beaks. One of these pterosaurs was *Eudimorphodon,* which looked a lot like a bat. It had a furry body and leathery wings. And it also had superpointy teeth, which it used for grabbing on tight to its prey.

Cockroaches survived the Permian–Triassic extinction—and every extinction after that. So did spiders, scorpions, and millipedes. Some

DOES THIS ANTEATER REMIND YOU OF ANYONE ... PREHISTORIC?

WHAT IS EVOLUTIONARY CONVERGENCE?

HAVE YOU NOTICED that when scientists describe prehistoric animals, they often compare them to modern animals, like hippos, shrews, or anteaters? They do that to make a quick distinction that everyone can understand. But there is also something called evolutionary convergence. This means that very early animals really did have physical traits that showed up in later animals. That includes dinosaurs and some of the animals that came before and after them. During the Triassic period, the reptile *Triopticus* had a domed head that was common in some of the dinosaurs that started to emerge after it, like some pachycephalosaurs.

ancestors of mammals were starting to emerge during this time, including a hippolike, car-size plant-eater with fat tusks called *Placerias*. One of the first true mammals also appeared in the Triassic: the furry four-foot (1.2-m)-long *Eozostrodon,* which some scientists compare in looks and size to a shrew.

Ferocious meat-eating predators were everywhere. *Postosuchus* was a fat-headed reptile that hunted in the woods on two legs. *Cynognathus* was a small but vicious four-legged predator that could easily chew through the tough skins of any poor plant-eater that crossed its path. *Drepanosaurus,* which looked like a cross between a chameleon and an anteater, was a reptile whose feet could grasp tree branches.

Finally, plonked down among all these other animals and plants, we come back around to the stars of our show: the dinosaurs. Truth be told, not many of the first Triassic dinosaurs were all that impressive to behold. Many were pretty small—especially compared to the behemoths that came later. They also weren't that diverse.

REPTILE *POSTOSUCHUS* ON THE HUNT

At first, they were mostly prosauropods—four- or two-legged saurischian herbivores that lived in the humid parts of Pangaea.

One of the earliest dinosaurs was *Eoraptor.* It lived 230 million years ago in what's now known as Argentina. A possible ancestor of giant sauropods like the titanosaurs, its name means "early plunderer." But it was on the small side—it grew to only three feet (0.9 m) long—and was shaped more like a minuscule *T. rex* than a *Brontosaurus,* for example. It was skinny and lightweight. It was also a nimble runner, moving quickly along on two feet through the desert where it lived. Most researchers list it as carnivorous, because it ate lizards and other small reptiles. But it may have also eaten plants, which would make it omnivorous.

Isanosaurus comes from what is now Thailand, where its fossilized bones were only recently found. This woods-dwelling, plump-bellied leaf-eater of the late Triassic may have been the first sauropod, a group that came after the prosauropods and directly descended from them. It had a pretty long tail, which it held high off the ground as it walked. From end to end, it measured a modest 20 feet (6.1 m). A line of spikes ran the length of its body, from the middle of its head all the way down its tail.

However, dinosaurs weren't exactly ruling the planet at this point. Some of the predatory dinosaurs were hunted by bigger reptiles from the crocodile line of archosaurs, for example. Some scientists have hypothesized that in order to survive during the Triassic, many dinosaurs hid out from other animals that wanted to eat them.

But once again, an extinction helped the dinosaurs. A big one happened 199 million years ago, at the end of the Triassic. This extinction killed off about 50 percent of all species on Earth. Lots of the crocodilian archosaurs were wiped out. So were many amphibians, including a "top predator" salamander relative called *Metoposaurus.*

Dinosaurs now had all the space and resources they needed to take over the planet.

ISANOSAURUS'S MOUTH WAS SUITED TO EATING LEAVES.

A MAMMAL-LIKE *DICYNODONT* (LEFT) AND AN *EORAPTOR* (RIGHT)

WITH A 33-FOOT (10.1-M) WINGSPAN, QUETZALCOATLUS MAY HAVE BEEN THE BIGGEST FLIER EVER.

PTEROSAURS

PTEROSAURS WERE THE MAIN FLYING ANIMALS during most of the Mesozoic era. They were not dinosaurs, but the two were closely related. Both were reptiles and archosaurs. And they had similar hips and ankles.

Some scientists think that a small, hopping insect-eater called *Scleromochlus* was a common ancestor to both pterosaurs and dinosauromorphs—the animals that eventually gave rise to the dinosaurs in the Triassic. But what, exactly, is a pterosaur?

"Winged lizard" pterosaurs took to the skies about 230 million years ago. That's 75 million years before birds evolved to join them in flight. Pterosaurs had hollow bones, which were light for flying. They had leathery membranes connecting the bones of their wings to their bodies but no feathers. Like the dinosaurs, they started out small in the Triassic. Their average wingspan was four feet (1.2 m). But they grew and grew, sometimes to enormous sizes, by the end of the Cretaceous. *Quetzalcoatlus* lived

PTEROSAURS, SUCH AS *TUPUXUARA*, MAY HAVE FED THEIR YOUNG AS BIRDS DO.

68 million years ago. With a 33-foot (10.1-m) wingspan, it may have been the biggest flier ever.

Some scientists think pterosaurs evolved into huge animals only after birds came on the scene. The theory is that, at first, birds and pterosaurs were about the same size, and they ate the same things. There weren't enough resources to go around for both of them. So pterosaurs evolved into larger fish-and-meat hunters that didn't compete with insect-eating birds.

Pterodactylus is probably the most famous of the pterosaurs. But it wasn't the only ptero-star.

- *Eudimorphodon:* One of the oldest pterosaurs, it had a long kite-like tail.
- *Ctenochasma:* Its 400 long, close-together teeth helped this wading pterosaur sieve out fish from rivers.
- *Gallodactylus:* This flier had a head crest, possibly to attract mates.

The Jurassic Period

Something really huge happened starting 200 million years ago. The continent of Pangaea had already begun to pull apart in the late Triassic. In the Jurassic period, it actually separated. The top half became the supercontinent Laurasia. This would eventually turn into North America, Europe, Russia, and Greenland. The bottom half drifted off into a super-continent called Gondwana. Far into the future, this would turn into South America, Africa, India, Australia, and Antarctica. There were two oceans now, the Pacific and the Tethys. Another strip of water ran between the two conti-nents, connecting the two oceans. This strip was called the proto–Atlantic Ocean. "Proto" means "coming before," and true to its name, this strip would eventu-ally become the Atlantic Ocean.

The desert in the middle part of Laurasia began to be taken over by shallow seas as the climate got warmer (although it would cool off toward the end of the Jurassic). The seas had islands popping up in their midst, formed by high waters flowing over land and, in some places, lava flowing from volcanoes that opened up as Earth's plates shifted to pull the continents apart.

Unlike many animal species, a lot of plants survived the Permian–Triassic extinction—especially conifers that looked a lot like the redwood trees, cypresses, and yews on our planet today. Ginkgoes, cycads, horse-tails, and ferns also thrived in the Jurassic, and forests grew lush. Mosses made a comeback. All these plants were great news for the humongous sauropods that were about to start busting out all over the planet.

Some amphibians and a lot of nondinosaur reptiles had vanished by the start of the Jurassic period. But there was still tons of life, with more coming all the time. Fast-swimming, dolphin-like ichthyo-saurs filled up the oceans. Fifty-foot (15.2-m) plesiosaurs with superlong necks snapped up unlucky fish for their dinners. Pliosaurs, with

LAURASIA AND GONDWANA IN THE EARLY JURASSIC.

WHIRINAKI FOREST PARK IN NEW ZEALAND FEATURES MODERN-DAY EXAMPLES OF CYCADS AND FERNS.

CONIFERS SURVIVED THE EXTINCTION.

45

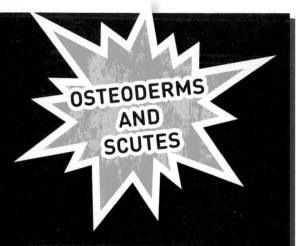

OSTEODERMS AND SCUTES

THESE TWO WORDS ARE SOMETIMES used interchangeably when people talk about the tough armor covering some of the dinosaurs. But they're not quite the same thing. Osteoderms are protective bones that grow right into skin. Scutes are outer coverings for osteoderms, sitting on top of those bones. They're made of keratin. That's the same substance found in human fingernails and animal horns.

THIS NODOSAUR FOSSIL IS SPECIAL BECAUSE OF THE PRESERVED DETAIL OF ITS OSTEODERMS AND SCUTES.

their short necks and wide mouths full of sharp teeth, were big and fierce enough to snack on plesiosaurs. Ammonites had spiral-shaped shells. Ancestors of sharks, rays, and squid were everywhere. Coral reefs thrived. And plankton was growing, including relatives of some kinds we have around today, like dinoflagellates, which glow like fireflies.

The first modern-style mammals appeared during this time. Not long after the Permian–Triassic extinction, a mouselike creature called *Megazostrodon* started prowling through the woods, hunting for insects—dragonflies, maybe, or mayflies—and spiders. Although *Megazostrodon* looked a lot like a mouse, it wasn't at all like a modern mammal—it laid eggs.

With this explosion of new life-forms, it didn't take long for the big sauropods, and those super-ferocious theropods that would eventually give us *T. rex,* to emerge. Right alongside them came the first of the "shield-bearing" thyreophorans, which include the stegosaurs and the ankylosaurs.

Now famous, *Stegosaurus* was heavy and thick all around. It was the length of a bus and weighed almost 14,000 pounds (6,350 kg). That

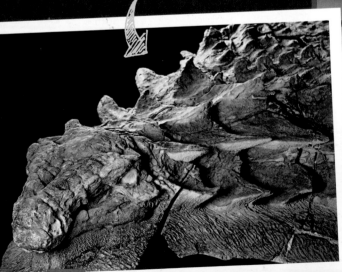

THE JURASSIC TEEMED WITH LIFE: *DIMORPHODON, MEGALOSAURUS,* AMMONITES, NAUTILUSES

massive body was controlled by a brain just a little bigger than a walnut!

Despite the fact that it ate low-lying plants like mosses and ferns and young trees (that's all it could reach with its short neck), *Stegosaurus* was a picture-perfect specimen of a Jurassic creature. It had a chunky, barrel-shaped body. Its tail ended in four thick, pointy spikes. One fossil of a carnivorous *Allosaurus* contained wounds from these spikes in it, so you can guess what their purpose was—*whack!* Running down its spine was *Stegosaurus*'s most famous feature of all, fin-shaped plates that stuck straight up from its back in a zigzag pattern. Scientists have several theories about what they were for. Some think they aided in defense, attracting mates. Others think they absorbed heat from the sun to keep it warm.

Ceratosaurus was a serious menace to the plant-eating *Stegosaurus*. This "horned lizard" theropod had—you guessed it—horns on its face. Three of them. It also had osteoderms—or protective bones in the skin—running down its back.

But it was *Allosaurus* that may have been the mightiest of *Stegosaurus*'s enemies. At 40 feet (12.2 m) long and 4,500 pounds (2,041 kg), it was smaller and lighter than the carnivores that would come after it. But it could still sink its sharp four-inch (10.2-cm)-long curved teeth and hooked claws into *Stegosaurus*'s flesh. In fact, its jaws could open extra wide—for extra-big and powerful bites. *Allosaurus* concentrated its bites on *Stegosaurus*'s neck, where there was a little less armor.

In addition to probably hunting alone, *Allosaurus* may have scavenged in packs, going out with a few others to pounce on weak or already-dead animals to share a feast. *Allosaurus* must have been fierce to look at. It had horns over its eyes, which it may have used as weapons. On top of that, it had strong arms with massive hooked claws at the ends and razor-sharp teeth that fell out and constantly

MASSIVE *STEGOSAURUS* HAD A BRAIN THE SIZE OF A WALNUT!

grew back in during its lifetime. Also, *Allosaurus* could run about 21 miles an hour (33.8 km/h). So it had no trouble catching up with the slow and plodding sauropods it preyed on.

Finally, no discussion of the Jurassic period would be complete without talking about creatures that could move through the air—and we don't mean the pterosaurs. We mean soaring dinosaurs! *Anchiornis* is the oldest soaring dinosaur found so far, in China. It lived about 161 million years ago. It was covered in feathers and grew to the size of a chicken. And like a chicken, it might not have been capable of true flight. Scientists think its feathers were too short for that. Instead, they imagine that it could glide from branch to branch,

MELANOSOMES FROM *ANCHIORNIS* FOSSILS HELPED SCIENTISTS LEARN THIS DINO'S COLORS.

like a flying squirrel might, catching insects in its beak as it leapt. Some scientists think that *Anchiornis* was black and gray with a red-feathered crest on its head. They figured this out by studying its melanosomes. Those are sacs within cells that store pigments, or colors.

Ten million years after *Anchiornis* came *Archaeopteryx*. Scientists agree it was a dinosaur— but was it also a bird? It may have been the first! But scientists cannot agree on that. On the one hand, *Archaeopteryx* had teeth and a long bony tail, just like any other theropod. It had claws on its wings, which is not exactly birdlike. But *Archaeopteryx* also had some of the characteristics of modern birds, like feathers, wings, and a wishbone. And it could fly! Paleontologists have studied about 12 *Archaeopteryx* skeletons found in Germany. They could see that its feathers were specially adapted to taking to the skies. And so were some of its muscles and ligaments, which would have given it the power to lift off the ground.

Right in the middle of this explosion of life, another extinction occurred, toward the end of the Jurassic period. This extinction happened 145 million years ago, and it mostly wiped out species that were living in the oceans. But on land, going into the Cretaceous period, dinosaurs were about to start getting bigger, more plentiful, and more varied.

ALLOSAURUS PROBABLY HUNTED ALONE BUT SCAVENGED IN PACKS.

MONSTERS OF THE SEA

BIG SWIMMING ANIMALS dominated the seas starting right after the Great Dying at the end of the Permian period. That's when some land animals took to the water and became the Triassic's ichthyosaurs. These reptiles gave birth out in the open seas and ranged in length from 30 inches (76.2 cm) to 72 feet (21.9 m). That's almost as big as a blue whale.

Later, at the beginning of the Jurassic, more land reptiles took the plunge and evolved into plesiosaurs with long necks and flippers. These creatures laid eggs out of the water on sandy beaches, much like sea turtles do today.

Both ichthyosaurs and plesiosaurs had to come up from the deep to breathe air. So did mosasaurs, the next version of sea monsters that emerged during the Cretaceous.

These strong-swimming creatures of the deep were top predators that ate squid, plesiosaurs, and even other mosasaurs. Upon finding the first mosasaur

A FISH FEAST FOR MOSASAURUS

fossils in the 18th century, scientists couldn't decide whether they belonged to a whale or a crocodile. That should give you an idea of what it looked like, with a fatty body, flippers, a long tail, and a narrow snout filled with teeth—including some running down the roof of its mouth. The most famous of the mosasaurs was *Mosasaurus*, which grew to 50 feet (15.2 m) in length. Its powerful jaws—the most powerful among the mosasaurs—could clamp down on giant sea turtles, shells and all.

The Cretaceous Period

All kinds of cool stuff happened in the Cretaceous period. Starting 145 million years ago, Earth really started to look like a planet humans would recognize! The supercontinents kept drifting away from each other. As they moved, they broke apart into smaller landmasses. Gondwana was now South America, Africa, and India. A fourth continent would later pull off and form Antarctica and Australia. Laurasia was now North America and a giant continent called Eurasia—basically, Europe and Asia. The five oceans were the Pacific, Arctic, North Atlantic, South Atlantic, and Tethys.

The breaking up of the continents was important. It helped all different kinds of life to start springing up all over Earth. This happened

as new ecosystems on those continents adapted to changing climates and land features. These climates made it possible for new species to evolve, including lots of dinosaur species.

More species of mammals appeared, too. Mammals in the Triassic and Jurassic laid eggs. But some Cretaceous mammals may have been placental. That means babies grew inside their mothers' wombs and were born live, not pushed out as eggs that needed to hatch. Many of them resembled the furry rodents we see these days, with pointy faces and long tails. Some of them may have even eaten small dinosaurs.

In the Cretaceous, bird-line dinosaurs—the line of dinosaurs that would eventually evolve into birds—became more and more diverse.

A HERD OF *PACHYRHINOSAURUS* THUDDING THROUGH GRASS

Actual crocodiles—not just crocodile ancestors—began lurking in rivers and lakes. Here's where life gets *really* good for dinosaurs. Sure, there were fewer of the stars of the Triassic and the Jurassic around—fewer sauropods, allosaurs, and stegosaurs. But other dinosaur groups were booming. Feathered theropod dromaeosaurs. The bony-headed ceratopsians. Duck-billed hadrosaurs. Thick-headed pachycephalosaurs. The world's most humongous animals, the titanosaurs. Predatory abelisaurs. And of course, the tyrannosaurs.

There were so many different kinds of dinosaurs in the Cretaceous that it's hard to know where to start talking about them. Take *Alxasaurus*. Even scientists think this dinosaur is odd. When you see *Alxasaurus* pictured in books, it looks like something out of a kids' puppet show. *Alxasaurus* weighed 750 pounds (340 kg) and stood 12 feet (3.7 m) tall on its two legs. Its body and two large, claw-tipped wings were covered in shaggy featherlike filaments. It was a theropod, but it ate plants. It was part of a group that would develop throughout the Cretaceous called the therizinosaurs, which included *Therizinosaurus,* the "scythe lizard," named for its long, thresher-like claws.

These weren't the only strange birdlike dinosaurs to come about in the Cretaceous. There were also the bizarre, ostrichlike ornithomimosaurs. The ornithomimosaurs got their name because they look like—or mimic—birds (*ornitho* means "bird" in Greek). They mostly looked like ostriches, and the "ostrich mimic" *Struthiomimus* may be the most ostrichlike of them all. It evolved about 76 million years ago, in the late Cretaceous, walking through the flatlands of Canada on its powerful legs. Its front wings had three clawed fingers on them. It may have used all its fingers for grabbing

SCIENTISTS AGREE THAT *ALXASAURUS* WAS ONE ODD DINOSAUR!

HOW FAST IS FAST? FOR *STRUTHIOMIMUS,* POSSIBLY 30 MILES AN HOUR (48 KM/H)!

things, like you use your hands. With its pointy beak on the end of its long neck, it nipped at shrubs, fruits, and nuts, and it also gobbled some small animals. This critter had no teeth in its beak, but some earlier ornithomimosaurs did—anywhere from just a few, all the way up to 230.

Deinocheirus lived a little later than *Struthiomimus,* in what is now Mongolia. At first, the only parts of this "terrible hand lizard" that were discovered were some eight-foot (2.4-m)-long arms. But later fossil discoveries helped scientists figure out some of *Deinocheirus*'s other features. It had a big hump in its back, short hind legs, and a duck-billed face. Scientists also think it may have run along the ground like the birds you see rushing in and out of the surf at the beach. It may have eaten fish in addition to plants.

When looking at artists' drawings of *Deinocheirus,* you can see how the ornithomimosaurs were related to the tyrannosaurs. They belong to the same clade. That means they share a common ancestor. At 36 feet (11 m) long and 12,000 pounds (5,443 kg), this massive feathered animal was pretty good competition for *T. rex* for the title of biggest theropod.

BIRDS ARE DINOS

HAS ANYONE EVER TOLD YOU that dinosaurs are not extinct? That's not just wishful thinking. It's the truth! Dinosaurs still live among us—in birds. Possibly because of the special way they evolved around 150 million years ago, birds were the only dinosaurs to survive the mass extinction.

You might be wondering, how, exactly, are birds dinosaurs? The story begins with carnivorous theropods. About 160 million years ago, birds split off into their own particular theropod group—the bird-line dinosaurs. Back in the early Jurassic, their ancestors had already started developing features like a wishbone. But little by little, they evolved even more. They got smaller and lighter. Their toothy snouts turned into toothless beaks. Their arms and hands turned into wings. Feet that could run turned into feet that could grasp when they perched. And finally, their feathers went from keeping them warm to helping them glide and then fly.

THAT'S RIGHT— THIS EMU IS A DINO, TOO.

How do we know all this? The fossil record shows us a direct line from feathered, flightless *Deinonychus* to feathered, gliding *Archaeopteryx* and to the 10,000 bird species that currently fly on our planet. Research shows that the modern birds that have the most in common with their prehistoric theropod ancestors are chickens and turkeys.

This theory about birds being dinosaurs was first proposed in the 1860s by a biologist named Thomas Henry Huxley. And it's been supported by science for almost 160 years!

"QUICK THIEF" *VELOCIRAPTOR* GNASHED MEAT WITH ITS 60 TEETH.

SCIENTISTS THINK *DEINONYCHUS* LIVED AND HUNTED IN PACKS, AMBUSHING PREY LIKE LIONS DO.

The dromaeosaurids were another birdlike group. *Utahraptor* was the biggest of the dromaeosaurids. And four-winged *Microraptor* was the smallest. There was also *Deinonychus,* which some scientists argue is the most important dinosaur fossil ever found. When it was discovered in 1960, scientists realized that many of their previous assumptions about dinosaurs were untrue. First of all, they learned dinosaurs didn't necessarily move slowly and sluggishly. Some dinosaurs could quickly chase down their prey. Next, they found strong links between dromaeosaurs and birds. These include the shapes of their necks, the large eye openings in their skulls, and their long arms and clawed hands.

"Terrible claw" *Deinonychus* did indeed have some terrible, sickle-shaped claws on its fingers. It also had "killing claws" on the second toes of its feet. These were useful for slashing at prey or holding it still. Needless to say, *Deinonychus* was a powerful predator, like all the members of its clade. It may also have been social. Scientists think it lived and hunted in packs, ambushing prey like lions do.

Another important dromaeosaur was *Velociraptor*. This "quick thief" from what is now Mongolia evolved 40 million years later than *Deinonychus*. It was a little smaller—seven feet (2.1 m) instead of 10 feet (3 m) long—and it weighed a little over 30 pounds (13.6 kg). It had nearly 60 supersharp, serrated teeth gnashing in its long jaws. There was plenty of meat for it to eat in the Cretaceous, such as bugs, frogs, smaller dinosaurs, reptiles, mammals, and pterosaurs—you name it. And it had feathers, even though it couldn't fly. Its feathers may have helped it stay warm, attract mates, or even protect its eggs.

Velociraptor was part of another famous fossil find called "Fighting Dinosaurs." In 1971, paleontologists dug up a *Velociraptor* from the middle of the Gobi. What was unusual about it was that it had one of its killer claws stuck into the neck of a *Protoceratops*. And the *Protoceratops* had its plant-munching teeth sunk into *Velociraptor*'s arm. The find was amazing and unexpected. But scientists don't think it shows a normal slice of Cretaceous life. Why? Because sheep-size *Protoceratops* might have been too big to be *Velociraptor*'s normal prey. They think *Velociraptor* may have attacked because it was desperate and starving. Or possibly because it was a young and foolish teenager, testing the limits of its abilities!

Confuciusornis is another feathered theropod of the Cretaceous. But it belongs to the Avialae clade. Included in that group are the birds flying around our parks and backyards today. One-foot (0.3-m)-long—you could say, bird-size—*Confuciusornis* had a thick, pointy beak, and wings and feathers shaped for flying. But it may have been an awkward flier. Its shoulders were the wrong shape for it to be graceful in the air, and its chest muscles weren't sturdy enough. The tails of the males had two long feathers streaming behind them. Living about 125 million years ago, *Confuciusornis* left behind so many fossils around one prehistoric lake in China that scientists think they must have congregated in giant flocks.

It may seem hard to believe that these birdlike animals were related to the tyrannosaurs. But they were all lizard-hipped saurischians to begin with, as well as being meat-eating predator theropods. They were also linked by the fact that they had feathers.

Early Cretaceous tyrannosaur *Yutyrannus* had feathers. At 125 million years old, *Yutyrannus* is an older relative to late Cretaceous *T. rex*. But it

CONFUCIUSORNIS FOSSIL FROM THE EARLY CRETACEOUS

helped scientists consider whether *T. rex* may have had feathers, too. (The short answer: maybe.) *Yutyrannus* stood on two scaly, clawed feet and had short arms with claws at the ends of them. It had strong jaws, with sharp little teeth, and a thick tail. It was kind of medium-size, compared to *T. rex,* at 5,000 pounds (2,268 kg) and 30 feet (9.1 m) long. But it may have been the largest feathered animal ever to live on the planet. The feathers covering it head to toe were fuzzy, like those on a newly hatched chick.

Tyrannosaurs evolved into bigger, sturdier animals as the Cretaceous chugged along. They may have even evolved so that only their babies had feathers, to keep them warm. That means they could have shed them

PROTOCERATOPS VS. VELOCIRAPTOR: WHO WILL WIN?

as they got older. Fuzzy *T. rex* babies? It's possible (if not quite adorable). But scientists aren't sure yet about the feathery status of a brand-new type of tyrannosaur that was found in southern China in 2014, and studied and named by National Geographic explorer Steve Brusatte! It has a nickname: Pinocchio rex. Yes, it had a long nose!

Qianzhousaurus—that's it actual scientific name—lived at the same time as *T. rex*. But they didn't compete for food. *T. rex* lived in North America, and *Qianzhousaurus* lived in Asia. Also, *Qianzhousaurus*'s unusually long snout meant it ate different, smaller stuff—maybe even fish—and its teeth couldn't chomp through bones. It also had an unusual line of small horns running down its nose. What's cool about this find is that it has made scientists reconsider some earlier tyrannosaur fossils they dug up. They used to think the long snouts on those tyrannosaurs—called *Alioramus*—got shorter as they grew into adults. Now they know that *Qianzhousaurus* and *Alioramus* belong to a new clade of long-snouted dinos.

Tyrannosaurs weren't the only fast, strong, meat-eating predators around. There were also the abelisaurs. But while the tyrannosaurs lived on the northern continents, the abelisaurs dominated the southern ones—their fossils have been found in Morocco, Argentina, and Madagascar. They were different from the tyrannosaurs in another way. Scientists think that as the tyrannosaurs got bigger, they started to lose horns and other ornaments on their heads. But as abelisaurs evolved, they developed bigger and

fancier head ornaments. Something they didn't develop, though, were longer arms. Most of the abelisaurs had puny ones.

The first abelisaur found by paleontologists was *Abelisaurus*. It lived about 85 million years ago in South America. It had no head ornaments at all. *Majungasaurus* lived 70 million years ago in Madagascar. It had only one little breakable horn sticking out of its head—too brittle to even fight with. But it also had an extra-thick skull. *Rajasaurus*, the king of lizards, was found in India and also dates to about 70 million years ago. It had a single small horn on the top of its skull, on the bone above the snout. Its cousin from Argentina, *Carnotaurus*, had bigger, thicker, meaner-looking horns over its eyes. It was also protected by prickly osteoderms that stuck out all over its body.

These carnivores were all fierce enough to take on the titanosaurs. In fact, abelisaurs, like *Abelisaurus*, were the main predators of *Saltasaurus*. Okay, at only 40 feet (12.2 m) long and 14,000 pounds (6,350 kg), *Saltasaurus* was not the biggest of this group. But it sure would have been a mouthful for 24-foot (7.3-m), 3,200-pound (1,451-kg) *Abelisaurus*—especially since it was also covered in armored osteoderms. But although *Abelisaurus* may have been able to chow down on a *Saltasaurus* now and then, the biggest of the titanosaurs were too big for it to eat.

There's a theory that the titanosaurs evolved into bigger and bigger animals alongside the ever-bigger theropods that wanted to eat them. If they were doing this to survive, it worked! Other sauropods like the diplodocids and the brachiosaurids may have gone extinct before

CARNOTAURUS HAD OSTEODERMS ALL OVER ITS BODY.

TITANOSAURS COULD STRIP BARK FROM TREES OR SWALLOW BRANCHES WHOLE.

THE MASSIVE ARGENTINOSAURUS

the end of the Cretaceous. But the titanosaurs thrived all the way to the end. Their fossils have been found on pretty much every continent. The *Patagotitan,* for example, had no predators whatsoever. This allowed the titanosaur group to become the most diverse and longest lived of the sauropods.

They ranged in size from 122 feet (37.2 m) long and 170,000 pounds (77,111 kg) to 24 feet (7.3 m) long and a mere 3,400 pounds (1,542 kg). Some had short legs and normal-size necks. Others had slender necks that stretched much longer than their bodies. A few were kind of duck-billed, but most of them had wide, short snouts. Since they were so big and needed to eat so much plant matter just to get through a single day, they were constantly adapting to eating many different things in many different ways. They could reach high or low for leaves or cones. They could strip bark from trees or swallow branches whole. It's also partly thanks to titanosaurs that we know there

HADROSAUR SKULL

was grass in the Cretaceous. That's because their coprolites—fossilized poop—contained several species of grass. Scientists once thought that grass didn't emerge until the Cenozoic era.

While the titanosaurs clomped around on four short, heavy legs and feet as plump as ottomans, another important group of Cretaceous herbivores got around on two legs, with feet that resembled camel feet. These were the hadrosaurs. You might know them better as the duck-billed dinosaurs. Yes, they had beaks. But behind those beaks were complicated, superstrong teeth specially made to grind up fibrous plants that were otherwise hard to digest. The more these teeth chomped, the more they changed their shape to become even better at chomping. And those teeth—hundreds of them—were constantly growing in.

About half the hadrosaurs were just regular old duckbills—plain hadrosaurines. The other half had crests on their skulls. These animals

NORTHERNMOST DINO, *UGRUNAALUK*

THE FRILL ON *PARASAUROLOPHUS* MAY HAVE MADE NOISE.

were called lambeosaurines. Their crests could be pretty spectacular, with small or large lumps, unicorn-like horns, wide frills or fins, or long swoops. These crests might not have been just for show. In fact, scientists think they served a very specific function: to make noise! That's because these dinosaurs' nasal passages actually looped up into these crests. This would have let the lambeosaurines make deep, loud vibrating sounds. Was it to warn each other of predators? Keep tabs on their herd members? Attract other cute lambeosaurines? Scientists are still working out those theories.

Maiasaura is a hadrosaurine from the late Cretaceous. Its name means "good mother lizard." At 30 feet (9 m) long, *Maiasaura* was among the largest of the hadrosaurs—and a pretty plain-looking one at that. No big crests, no frills, it was a typical hadrosaurine. *Maiasaura* eventually went extinct, leaving room for *Edmontosaurus,* a bigger hadrosaurine cousin, to have the run of North America. In 2015, paleontologists reported that they'd found a new kind of hadrosaur called *Ugrunaaluk* ... in Alaska, U.S.A. This dinosaur is now a record-holder. So far, it's the most northerly dinosaur ever found and probably got snowed on.

Parasaurolophus was an über-lambeosaurine, with one of the most whimsical head frills of all.

The frill was fused to its nose and swooped back and over its head. It may also be the best example of how a hadrosaur crest could have been used to make noise. With tubes extending all the way through its crest, it sort of resembled a trumpet. Did it sound like one, too?

Scientists don't know what noises were made by other types of dinosaurs with oddly shaped heads, called the pachycephalosaurs. These late Cretaceous bonehead dinosaurs had skulls that were sometimes 16 inches (40.6 cm) thick. That's 20 times thicker than paleontologists have found on other dinosaurs. Scientists even named one of them Knucklehead, or *Colepiocephale.*

What would pachycephalosaurs have needed boneheads for? The leading theory is for head-butting other dinosaurs. Which apparently became more necessary as the pachycephalosaurs evolved, because one of the earliest ever found, 76-million-year-old *Goyocephale*, had only a slightly thick head. Whereas 66- to 70-million-year-old *Pachycephalosaurus* had a dome that was eight to 10 inches (20 to 25 cm) thick sitting on top of its head like a cap. This cap was also ringed by short, spiky horns, which extended down its nose.

Pachycephalosaurus, which grew to only about 15 feet (4.6 m), had another cool feature: its teeth. Some of them were typical leaf-eating teeth that were tucked in behind their beaks. But *Pachycephalosaurus* also had other teeth in its cheeks, which might have helped it to grind up foods like nuts and fruit.

After the early Cretaceous, the heads of ceratopsians started to really branch out! Seventy-five million years ago, *Protoceratops* was eight feet (2.4 m) tall and 183 pounds (83 kg), with cheek horns and a massive frill growing out of the back of its head. Four-ton (3.6 t) *Pachyrhinosaurus*, which lived in North America 73–69 million years ago, also had a big frill at the back of its head. But even more impressive, it had a massive bone called a boss covering the whole top of its nose, and a second boss higher up, over its eyes. It was

STYGIMOLOCH (LEFT) HAD PLAINER HEADGEAR THAN SOME OTHER PACHYCEPHALOSAURS.

neighbors with spiked lizard *Styracosaurus*, a massive ceratopsian with elaborate horns sticking out along the edges of its frill. These are called parietal horns. Styracosaurus also had another big horn sticking out of its nose, giving it the look of a prehistoric rhinoceros.

Scientists are certain that ceratopsians' head ornaments were used to attract mates and intimidate rivals, but they are not sure why they were so different among the species. One of the most interesting theories for the differences is that frills and horns let *Styracosaurus* recognize other *Styracosaurus*, and it also helped them recognize that *Protoceratops* was not a *Styracosaurus*. As paleontologists continue to find new ceratopsian fossils—and pachycephalosaur and hadrosaur fossils—little by little, they'll be able to piece together more answers.

SOUNDS OF THE DINOSAURS

PACHYCEPHALOSAURS MAY HAVE MADE trumpet noises through their head ornaments. But what did other dinosaurs sound like? In the movies, dinosaurs usually roar. But according to new research, they may really have sounded like a cross between a crocodile and a bird.

The sound they probably made is called a closed-mouth vocalization. You hear birds like doves making this kind of sound when they coo from their neck area. They do this by pushing air down into a pouch in their esophagus. Crocodiles can do this, too—with much louder results! And dinosaurs may have been loudest of all. Which birds would dinosaurs have sounded most like? The best guess of scientists is the biggest of the birds—ostriches and cassowaries.

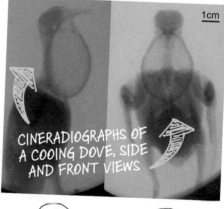

1cm

CINERADIOGRAPHS OF A COOING DOVE, SIDE AND FRONT VIEWS

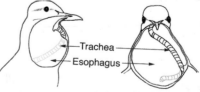

Trachea
Esophagus

DIG IN

ON TRACK

TRACKWAYS ARE IMPORTANT TO PALEONTOLOGISTS for identifying which dinosaurs roamed Earth, and where.

Using the field guide at the right, see if you can identify the tracks of the various dinosaurs in the photos below. Then use what you know about these dinos to create a realistic story about what was going on here: Were these dinosaurs meat- or plant-eaters? Were they all adults? How big do you think they were? Why had they all come to this one particular area? Were they all here at the same time?

On a separate piece of paper, draw the scene your story suggests. Research what other animals and plants might be in the scene, and add them to your art, just like a real paleoartist would!

1. MÜNCHEHAGEN, GERMANY

2. DINOSAUR RIDGE, COLORADO, U.S.A.

3. MOENAVE FORMATION, ZION NATIONAL PARK, UTAH, U.S.A.

DINO TRACK FIELD GUIDE

ALLOSAURUS

DILOPHOSAURUS

DEINONYCHUS

IGUANODON

TYRANNOSAURUS

APATOSAURUS

TRICERATOPS

DIPLODOCUS

STEGOSAURUS

VELOCIRAPTOR

ANKYLOSAURUS

GALLIMIMUS

ANSWER KEY: 1. Researchers believe these tracks were made by a Diplodocus. 2. There are two types of dino tracks: *Iguanodon* and *Gallimimus*. 3. Researchers believe these tracks came from a *Dilophosaurus*.

CHAPTER 3
THE LIVES OF DINOSAURS

TRICERATOPS THRIVED DURING THE LATE CRETACEOUS.

INTRODUCTION

THE BEAUTIFUL ISLE OF SKYE IS ENCHANTING GREEN COUNTRYSIDE

off the coast of Scotland, with towering mountains and peat-clogged streams.

STEVE BRUSATTE

It's also one of the best locations in the world to find fossils from the middle part of the Jurassic.

When I was there in 2015, I went to a site on the far northeastern side of the island, near the ruins of a castle. That was where a geologist friend had been making maps of the rocks. He had found a small bone that I could see had tooth sockets. It turned out to be a piece of the jaw of a small, dog-size crocodile that paddled in the lagoons 170 million years ago. After seeing the jawbone, I thought, *I've gotta go back and see if there are any more of these!*

I didn't find more croc bones, but I did find fish bones and shark teeth. For several hours one day, my students and I were on our hands and knees, collecting teeth. The sun started to set, it was getting cold, and the wind was picking up. It was time to call it a day.

The students packed up and went to the vehicles. I stayed behind with a fellow paleontologist, Tom Challands. We collected our gear and walked across the tidal platform.

That's when we saw these weird, tire-size circular depressions in the rock. We looked closer and realized they were not entirely circular but had bits sticking out of them that looked like toes. In some cases, there were pairs of depressions, both big and small, and that's when we knew they were the tracks of dinosaurs—and not just any dinosaurs, but the biggest of them all: sauropods. The more we looked, the more we started to see them everywhere!

The students and I spent the next few days mapping the area. We discovered three layers of these sauropod tracks in the lagoon and in rock formations found in pretty shallow water. That was unusual, and it completely broke my image of sauropods as creatures thundering across the land, creating earthquakes and kicking up dust. It turned out that they were also at home near the shore. Why? Was there lots of food there? Or was it to escape predators?

It's hard to be sure, but what's so cool about this find is that these were the first sauropod trackways found in Scotland, and because of this we know they were utterly dominant and living in different environments.

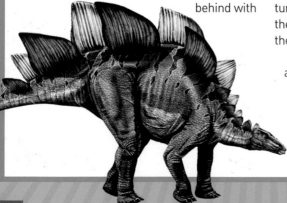

SAUROPOD FOOTPRINTS IN SCOTLAND

STEVE OBSERVES SMALL FOSSILS PRESERVED IN THE SAME LAYER AS DINOSAUR FOOTPRINTS ON SKYE.

WE SAW THESE WEIRD, TIRE-SIZE CIRCULAR DEPRESSIONS IN THE ROCK.

STEVE (RIGHT) WITH COLLEAGUE TOM CHALLANDS, SURROUNDED BY PAIRS OF DEPRESSIONS

FOOTPRINTS

WHAT WAS IT LIKE TO BE A DINOSAUR?

On the surface, it might seem that dinosaurs don't have much in common with you. They weren't mammals. They didn't have to clean their bedrooms. And they're, well, mostly dead. But while they were alive, they had to follow certain rules of existence that apply to all animals.

SCRAPES, POSSIBLY FROM DINO MATING DANCES

In order for any species to live, and go on living, animals have to mate and have babies. Those babies have to grow up and repeat the process, for as long as possible. This was a fact of life for dinosaurs, too.

Dinosaur Moms and Dads

Let's say you're a dinosaur that wants to tell another cute dinosaur you're available. How do you get that message across? You don't offer flowers, and you can't send a text message. New evidence suggests that some dinosaurs danced. Males trying to impress females may have pranced around and dug at the dirt with their feet. This made deep, weird-looking tracks called scrapes. Scientists have found these types of markings in Colorado and other dinosaur sites in the western United States. The marks look similar to nestlike holes made by

THEROPOD MATING DANCES MAY HAVE LOOKED SOMETHING LIKE THIS.

birds today trying to impress females—except that they're huge. Some of the fossilized scrapes are the size of bathtubs.

But there was probably more than one way for dinosaurs to show off to potential mates. Male theropods like *Gorgosaurus* and *Sinraptor* may have bitten other males in the face to show potential girlfriends who was biggest and strongest, and therefore worthy of being a dad. *Triceratops* males may have locked horns, like deer or antelope do, to impress females they were interested in. Some other dinosaurs had unusual features that weren't sturdy or practical enough to use defensively or to catch prey. So scientists hypothesize that these features had something to do with mating rituals. They include things like hadrosaurs' big, elaborate crests, some of which may also have been eye-catchingly colorful, which would have made a hadrosaur look bigger and more attractive.

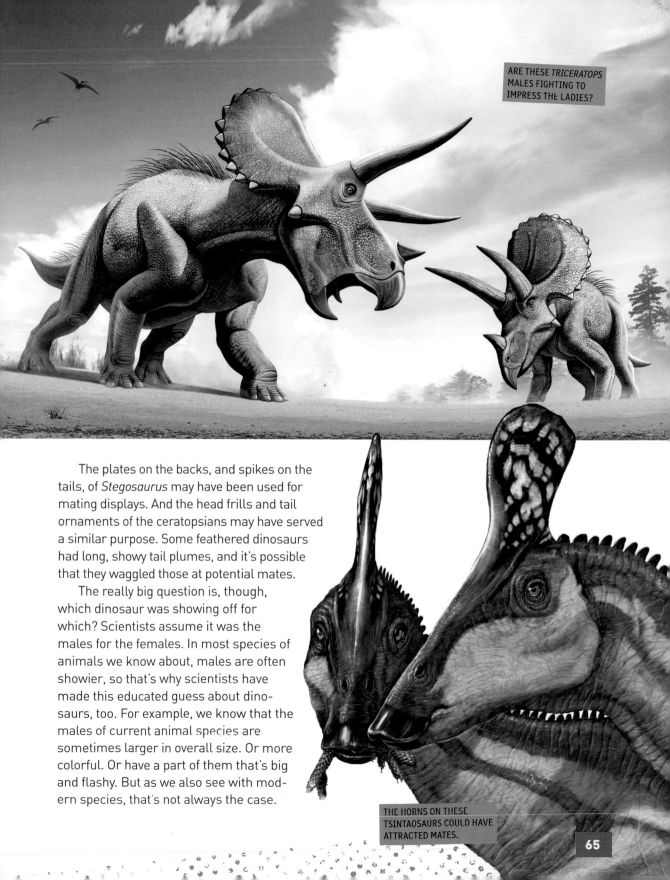

ARE THESE *TRICERATOPS* MALES FIGHTING TO IMPRESS THE LADIES?

The plates on the backs, and spikes on the tails, of *Stegosaurus* may have been used for mating displays. And the head frills and tail ornaments of the ceratopsians may have served a similar purpose. Some feathered dinosaurs had long, showy tail plumes, and it's possible that they waggled those at potential mates.

The really big question is, though, which dinosaur was showing off for which? Scientists assume it was the males for the females. In most species of animals we know about, males are often showier, so that's why scientists have made this educated guess about dinosaurs, too. For example, we know that the males of current animal species are sometimes larger in overall size. Or more colorful. Or have a part of them that's big and flashy. But as we also see with modern species, that's not always the case.

THE HORNS ON THESE TSINTAOSAURS COULD HAVE ATTRACTED MATES.

65

A MALE *STEGOSAURUS* MAY HAVE HAD TALL FINS.

One problem with trying to figure out the details of dino lives is that we don't always have enough complete fossils of each species for scientists to know for sure if the dinosaur with the bigger head crest or the longest tail feathers is a male or a female. Little by little, though, scientists have pieced together some clues.

In 2005, researchers reported that a *T. rex* specimen found in Montana, U.S.A., had a special substance in its thighbone called medullary bone, which is present only in female birds. That meant the *T. rex* specimen was a female. Medullary bone has lots of calcium in it, which female birds use for making eggshells. Since then, scientists have found medullary bone in *Allosaurus* and *Tenontosaurus* specimens, and they're actively on the hunt for it in other dinosaur species as well. Now that they know what to look for, scientists hope to solve

SLICE OF *T. REX* BONE SHOWING OUTER CORTICAL BONE (CB) SURROUNDING THE MEDULLARY BONE (MB)

MB

CB

the male versus female riddle for many more dinosaur types.

Another clue comes from *Stegosaurus.* Scientists once thought that there were two different species of *Stegosaurus:* those with tall plates running down their backs, and those with wider, bigger fins. But in 2015, scientists realized that every single piece of these dinosaurs was the same *except* for those fins. So they made an educated guess about what they thought was actually going on: The female *Stegosauruses* had one kind of fin, and the males had another.

In 2016, British paleontologists figured out that adult *Protoceratops* had bigger head frills than juveniles did. This told them that their frills grew as they reached mating age. And this in turn meant it was likely that the frills were used to attract members of the opposite sex. But who had the bigger frills—males or females? Scientists haven't worked that out yet.

A *MAIASAURA* MOM FEEDS HER YOUNG.

EGG TIMER

ONE THING SCIENTISTS DO KNOW is how long it took for dinosaur eggs to hatch. How did they figure it out? Dinosaur embryos! That is, fossilized baby dinosaurs that were found inside fossilized eggs.

Researchers conducted studies on embryos from three-ounce (85-g) *Protoceratops* eggs and from almost nine-pound (4.1-kg) *Hypacrosaurus* eggs. They were most interested in looking at the embryos' teeth. It turns out that teeth show growth lines like the growth rings inside tree trunks. These lines let scientists count how old the embryos were. With that information, they could estimate how much time would have been left till the embryos hatched. The overall hatching time turned out to be three months for the small *Protoceratops* eggs and six months for the basketball-size *Hypacrosaurus* eggs.

Starting Out in Life

All dinosaurs began as eggs, laid in clutches, or groups, by their mothers in nests. And just like the dinosaurs themselves, these nests varied. Some were big mounds of earth with bowl-shaped depressions in the center—and the bigger the dinosaur, the bigger the nest. The biggest dinosaurs laid 20 or more eggs. Sometimes the clutches of eggs were arranged in a circle, and sometimes they were laid out in a straight line. If the dinosaur was too big to sit on the eggs without breaking them, they might have covered them with moss and leaves and branches to keep them warm until they hatched.

Some dinosaurs, including the hadrosaurs, nested in great big colonies. They'd come back to the same nests to lay their eggs year after year. And although they were too big for nest-sitting, parent hadrosaurs, like "good mother lizard" *Maiasaura,* rested near their nests to guard them from predator mammals and snakes. They also brought food to their babies once they hatched. Newborn hadrosaurs were too small and defenseless to fend for themselves.

PROTOCERATOPS HATCHING FROM ONE EGG IN A CLUTCH

RAHONAVIS USING RAPETOSAURUS AS A PERCH

A HUNGRY *RAPETOSAURUS* EATS NEAR A NEST OF HATCHING MAJUNGASAURS.

Other big dinosaurs, like the titanosaur *Rapetosaurus*, likely didn't stick around to watch its eggs open. Baby *Rapetosaurus* fossils show that these little seven-and-a-half-pound (3.4-kg) creatures hatched looking pretty much like a smaller version of the 37,000-pound (16,783-kg) adult *Rapetosaurus*, with their heads and bodies and limbs all showing the same proportions as the grown-ups'. This tells scientists that they were born ready to fend for themselves. The same may have been true for some of the nonbird theropods, which were equipped with big teeth and claws to help them survive, even as newborns.

Some smaller dinosaurs, such as *Oviraptor*, *Troodon*, and *Deinonychus*, more likely sat on their eggs to keep them warm. They would cover the nests with their own feathers, sometimes draping their wings over them. It's also likely that male *Troodons* and males from other species shared in this duty—just like we find with some species of birds today.

Scientists have also found evidence that *Maiasaura* moms and dads shared in taking care of their babies even after they were born—not only looking out for their safety but bringing them food and possibly teaching them how to hunt for themselves. Some kinds of dinosaurs, like *Psittacosaurus*, may have used teenage babysitters to take care of big groups of the very young dinosaurs in their herds. Among other types of herding dinosaurs, like theropod *Falcarius*, ceratopsian *Protoceratops*, and ankylosaur *Pinacosaurus*, young dinosaurs lived all together in groups called pods, away from the adults.

Surviving in the Wild

How dinosaurs lived once they were born depended very much on what kinds of dinosaurs they were. There was so much diversity among them. Many plant-eaters seem to have lived in

SMALL MEAT-EATERS, LIKE *VELOCIRAPTOR*, MAY HAVE HUNTED IN PACKS.

SAUROPODS STUCK TOGETHER FOR SAFETY.

herds. Paleontologists have found tracks showing many members of the same species walking together. They've also found bone beds containing fossilized remains of members of the same species, of all different ages. If they died together like this, they most certainly lived together, too.

Sticking together in a group was a safety tactic for species that were preyed upon. With predators on the prowl, just waiting for the chance to eat them, living in a herd would increase their chances of survival. It definitely paid to have lots of extra eyes on the lookout for an ambush!

Smaller meat-eaters may also have lived in packs, banding together in order to operate as more efficient hunters. Although a bunch of nine-foot (2.7-m)-long *Deinonychuses,* for example,

could have taken down a much bigger sauropod together, they wouldn't have been able to conquer one on their own.

Still other dinosaurs may have lived together as couples, raising their young, defending their territory, and feeding together. And dinosaurs of all ages might very well have enjoyed each other's company. In 2015, scientists found tracks they call *Megalosauripus* (that's right—tracks get their own names!) on a German beach. They could tell from looking at the footprints that two two-legged, medium-size carnivores had been out for a pleasant stroll. And that one was young, and the other older—perhaps a parent and child. This has helped researchers understand that even animals that didn't live in herds were social and in each other's company.

Dinosaurs Piece by Piece

For the most part, dinosaurs grew up pretty fast. That's partly because some of them had to take care of themselves right out of the egg. Paleontologists have found that dinosaurs reached full adult size and maturity anywhere between two years old (for a smallish *Psittacosaurus*) and 20 years old (for massive *Tyrannosaurus rex*).

Because dinosaurs mostly grew quickly, and also because birds are like dinosaurs and can tell us a lot about their extinct relatives, scientists started wondering if maybe dinosaurs were endothermic, or warm-blooded, after all.

Since dinosaurs are reptiles, scientists thought that meant they were also ectothermic, or cold-blooded. Lizards, snakes, fish, and frogs are all ectotherms. They warm their bodies mostly by basking in the sun or stretching out on warm rocks.

SCIENTISTS ONCE THOUGHT DINOS WERE ECTOTHERMS, LIKE NORTHERN CAIMAN LIZARDS.

Endothermic mammals, like humans, dogs, mice, and birds, get warmth from inside their bodies, and it's kept there by insulation—feathers, hair, and fur are all effective kinds of insulating materials. Since warmth translates into energy, ectotherms store up only enough heat to be active in short bursts. And because endotherms can generate their own heat, they're almost always ready for action. They can also do a lot of things quicker than ectotherms can, like grow to full size and digest their food.

To study the question, scientists analyzed soil from the Mesozoic era. This helped them estimate the temperature of the environment at various times throughout those 165 million years. They also analyzed dinosaur eggshells, to figure out the body temperatures of the dinosaurs that laid them. They learned

DINOSAURS WERE PROBABLY MESOTHERMIC, LIKE SHARKS.

that dinosaurs were neither warm- nor cold-blooded, but something in between: mesothermic.

A different study found that when it came to their thermostats, dinosaurs may have been a lot like great white sharks. Great white sharks are mostly cold-blooded. But when they need to chase down prey or escape a dangerous situation, the activity of their muscles heats up their blood. This gives them a burst of energy. They can hold on to the heat and energy they make for a little while, but they can't maintain their temperatures like we humans do. But sharks don't need to stay warm all the time. And maybe dinosaurs didn't need to, either.

Another part of dinosaurs that no one usually sees is their brains. That's because brains—like muscles, and other organs like hearts, livers, and intestines—are made of soft tissue. Unlike bones, soft tissue decomposes, or rots, instead of turning into fossils. So to learn about brains, scientists usually have to study the brain cavities in fossilized dinosaur skulls. And for a long time, scientists thought those brain cavities were pretty small, some even impossibly so. How could a brain the size of a walnut operate a dinosaur the size of a car?

In the 19th century, some scientists thought big dinos like *Camarasaurus* and *Stegosaurus* actually had two brains. One in their heads, and one in their butts. After all, they reasoned, those brain cavities were way too small! And down past the hips, some of these big dinosaurs had second, larger cavities the scientists couldn't explain. What if they were for holding a second brain? (The scientists politely called those second cavities posterior braincases.) A second brain would be able to control the whole bottom half of a dinosaur. Kind of like the second puppeteer works the back half of a horse costume. The

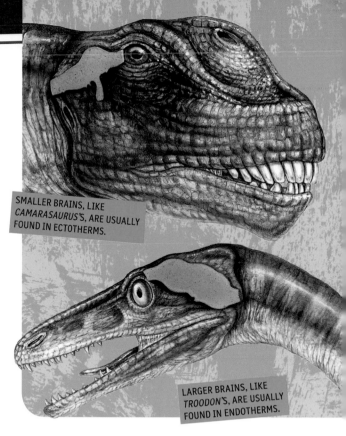

SMALLER BRAINS, LIKE *CAMARASAURUS'S*, ARE USUALLY FOUND IN ECTOTHERMS.

LARGER BRAINS, LIKE *TROODON'S*, ARE USUALLY FOUND IN ENDOTHERMS.

scientists thought a second brain would neatly explain some things about how dinosaurs functioned. But it turned out that the butt brain was not a brain at all but a big bundle of nerves. Dinosaurs had only one brain each. And even though the brains were sometimes very small, they were big enough to allow the dinosaurs to survive, and to thrive.

There was one problem with having a small brain in a big body, though. Big bodies generate a lot of heat. How did the big meat-eating dinosaurs manage their body temperatures to keep their brains from reaching sizzling temperatures? Scientists think they had a special system for cooling off. Their circulatory systems, which carried blood and oxygen all over their bodies, may have also dumped heat from their bodies into their nasal cavities before it could reach their brains and fry them. After all, dinosaurs had pretty basic needs: to eat, mate, and protect themselves. And to do that, they mostly relied on

APATOSAURUS TEETH WERE MADE FOR CHOMPING PLANTS.

their senses. In looking at the braincases of carnivorous dinosaurs, scientists noticed that they would have held really big olfactory lobes. These gave tyrannosaurs and other theropods a great sense of smell, so they could locate their prey. Meat-eaters had pretty good hearing and vision, too. These also would have helped them hunt down their dinner. All in all, carnivores had the biggest brains of the dinosaurs, with the smaller theropods like *Troodon* and *Velociraptor* being the smartest of all.

While the big meat-eaters had a good sense of smell, small herbivores had good eyesight. That's because they were especially vulnerable to attacks from carnivores, so they needed good eyesight to spot them. They may have needed to look out for them in the dark, too. Herbivores' braincases show that these dinosaurs had big eye sockets to hold eyes that could see in all directions.

Other dinosaur parts that paleontologists study and that give them important clues about how these creatures lived are their teeth. And some dinosaurs had lots and lots of teeth. They

COMPARE *T. REX'S* TOOTH (FAR LEFT) TO *CAMARASAURUS'S* (FAR RIGHT).

were mostly made from two hard materials called dentin and enamel. Because of this, they fossilized easily. In fact, for some dinosaur species, paleontologists have found only their teeth. But teeth are among the most important dinosaur pieces to study. They can tell us a lot about the animals that used them to bite, chew, and chomp.

Teeth can tell us whether dinosaurs were meat-, fish-, or plant-eaters—or if they were omnivores and ate a little of everything. They also tell us if dinosaurs ate low along the ground or nibbled high from the treetops, and if they chewed their food or swallowed it whole. They tell us about the habitat dinosaurs lived in and what kind of food supply existed there. They tell us how old they were when they died and how species evolved over vast amounts of time.

Some dinosaurs had just a few teeth working in their jaws at one time, and some had many. Some had only one kind of tooth, and others had several. Some had teeth positioned just at the fronts of their mouths. Some had teeth fully lining their top and bottom jaws. Some even had extra teeth in their cheeks. All these different kinds of teeth and groupings of teeth affected how and what a dinosaur could eat.

Almost all dinosaurs replaced their teeth periodically. When teeth became too worn down from use, they were pushed out of their sockets by new teeth waiting just behind them. That's one reason paleontologists find so many dinosaur teeth when they don't find many other fossils at all. Some dinosaurs had several thousand teeth in their head that they used, then lost, during their lifetimes.

Meat-Eaters and Fish-Eaters

The teeth inside the jaws of theropod predators had very specific shapes. But not all meat-eaters ate the same things, or ate in the same ways. Most carnivores generally had sharp, narrow, curved teeth that were serrated along both edges. That is, they were jagged like a saw or a bread knife. Teeth that curve backward, or recurve, are good for slashing at prey to weaken it, and also for slicing up meat. Many carnivores, like *Allosaurus* and *Carcharodontosaurus,* had serrated recurved teeth. These predators had as many as several dozen teeth in their jaws at one time, each one up to five inches (12.7 cm) long—or even longer.

Plant-Eaters and Omnivores

Of course, plant-eating dinosaurs were built to eat very different kinds of things than the carnivorous dinosaurs. These differences were apparent in their heads and teeth, too. For example, many of them had pouches in their cheeks, where they could store their food while they grazed. Different species also had more varieties of teeth types than the carnivores did, allowing them to grind, saw, or nip away at many different kinds of plant matter. Some even had several different kinds of teeth in their mouths at the same time. This helped them make the most of all the vegetation available to them.

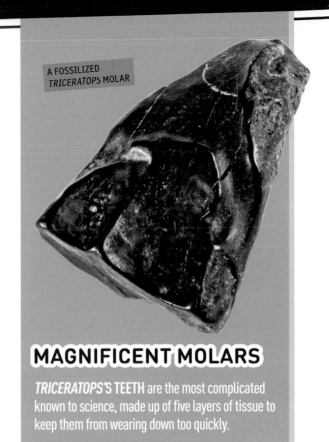

A FOSSILIZED *TRICERATOPS* MOLAR

MAGNIFICENT MOLARS

TRICERATOPS'S TEETH are the most complicated known to science, made up of five layers of tissue to keep them from wearing down too quickly.

HETERODONTOSAURUS HAD A BEAK AND THREE KINDS OF TEETH.

THE PROOF IS IN THE COPROLITES

HOW DO SCIENTISTS KNOW what dinosaurs ate? They follow the evidence! Dinosaur teeth reveal a lot about how and what they chewed. We can compare that knowledge against the fossil record for plants and prey animals that existed at the same time. Also, though very rarely, paleontologists find dinosaur fossils with their dinners still preserved in their stomachs. In 2012, they discovered two fuzzy-feathered early-Cretaceous *Sinocalliopteryx* with bellies full of *Confuciusornis* and an unidentified kind of dromaeosaur.

COPROLITES SHOW WHAT ANIMALS ATE.

The most common clue about what dinosaurs ate comes from their coprolites, or fossilized poop. There's a lot of this stuff around. But you have to know exactly what you're looking for, because most coprolites look like log-shaped pieces of rock. Scientists who've cracked them open for a peek inside have found all sorts of interesting fossilized things, like bones, muscle tissue, plants, leaves of flowering trees, bits of wood, and grasses. The only tricky part is figuring out which dinosaurs pooped out which kinds of digested food matter.

Lasting Impressions

Like dinosaur brains, most dinosaur skin was made of softer stuff than bone. It was often eaten, or it rotted away before it could create a fossil for us to one day see and study. For a long time, scientists and the paleoartists who make scientific drawings and models of dinosaurs had to study living, nonextinct animals in order to make educated guesses about what dinosaur skin might have looked like. But they had no way of knowing for certain how accurate their guesses were.

Luckily, for our understanding of the way dinosaurs looked on their outsides as well as their bone-filled insides, "often" is not the same as "always." And every

A FOSSILIZED IMPRESSION OF HADROSAUR SKIN

now and then throughout the years, paleontologists have found clues to the different kinds of wrappings that held dinosaur bones and muscles all together.

One way scientists can know what dinosaur skin looked like is from the impressions it made. If a dinosaur lay down or fell to the ground, the pattern of its skin could be pressed into the soft mud beneath it. Maybe the dinosaur got up and walked away, or maybe it was gobbled up by scavengers. But it left its markings behind in that mud. The mud turned slowly to rock. And the patterned rock became a fossil. Another way patterns can be preserved is by a cast or a mold, which works in a similar way. But in this case, mud may drip on

PALEOARTISTS

STEVE BRUSATTE

TO MAKE AN IMAGE of those Scottish sauropod tracks and to show what the lagoon might have been like, Tom Challands and I worked with a great Scottish artist named Jon Hoad. He's one of the best paleoartists in the world for setting a scene—not just with sauropods but also with other dinosaurs, animals, and plants. He actually knows a lot more about plants of the Jurassic than I do—he's a real specialist. The Isle of Skye in the middle of the Jurassic was an environment that was warm and wet and lush, but subjected to nasty storms. He put all that into the image, and we went back and forth talking about it. That's a cool process, mixing science with the creative side of things.

You can see the image he came up with here. It's kind of a postapocalyptic scene, a bad day on Skye. There's just been a big storm. There are a couple of sauropods wandering around, and dead logs and leaves and other things strewn at their feet. They've survived the storm, and they're looking for food. There are some pterosaurs up in the sky, catching the air currents and looking at the fish carcasses on the far shore, as wells as an early tyrannosaur looking at the sauropods and thinking, *Do I want to go into the water? Are they too big to eat?*

JON HOAD'S ART OF SAUROPODS MAKING TRACKS ACROSS THE ISLE OF SKYE

SCALY SKIN OF A TITANOSAUR

PROTECTIVE SCALES OF ANKYLOSAURUS ...

... AND OF TRICERATOPS

top of a dinosaur, filling in all the wrinkles and folds in its skin. Then, again, the mud turns to rock, and the image of the skin becomes a fossil.

From impressions and casts that paleontologists have found over the years, they've gotten some really good ideas of how certain dinosaur skins looked. They now know that dinosaurs had scaly skin and that, even though the patterns of skin were different depending on the dinosaur species, their scales were usually side by side, rather than overlapping each other the way they do on fish. They've also learned that *Diplodocus* had scales that were as tiny as pinheads. And the small, pebbly scales covering the body of *Edmontosaurus* had even smaller scales tucked in around them. *Psittacosaurus,* too, had round scales in all different sizes, covering it from head to toe. A newly found skin fossil from a titanosaur that lived in present-day Spain during the late Cretaceous showed what is now a flower-shaped scale pattern, with a big bump in the center surrounded by five or six smaller bumps. Impressions of titanosaur *Saltasaurus*'s skin shows that it had bony lumps covering its skin in a tough but flexible kind of body armor.

All these scales were protective in some way. They would have helped to keep dinosaurs from being bitten by insects, pricked by thorny shrubs, or punctured by the teeth of other hungry animals. And although tough skin was important, it was also important that it be flexible enough for the dinosaurs to move around easily. Scale patterns helped create that flexibility.

One exception to soft, decaying dinosaur skin was the hard armor that grew on dinosaurs like the ankylosaurs. The knobs and plates covering them were osteoderms, literally pieces of bone that grew in their skin. These were covered with scutes made of keratin—that's the same hard substance that makes up our fingernails and animal horns, and it's hard enough to fossilize.

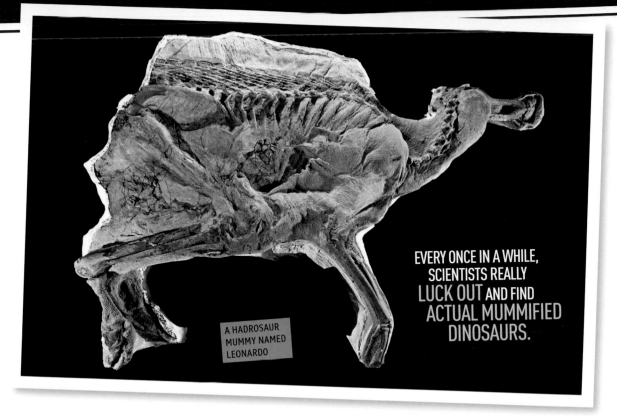

EVERY ONCE IN A WHILE, SCIENTISTS REALLY LUCK OUT AND FIND ACTUAL MUMMIFIED DINOSAURS.

A HADROSAUR MUMMY NAMED LEONARDO

Impressions of ankylosaur skin also exist, though, helping scientists to understand how scute-covered osteoderms were arranged in various patterns on dinosaur backs.

Every once in a while, scientists really luck out and find actual mummified dinosaurs. For dinosaurs to be completely preserved with their skin and other tissue, conditions have to be just right. Usually that means conditions need to be extremely dry with no oxygen circulating, because moisture and oxygen cause things to decay.

In 2001, paleontologists found an almost entire mummified hadrosaur in Montana, U.S.A. It showed impressions of skin all over the dinosaur—its legs, rib cage, neck, and one arm. Thanks to this dinosaur mummy, known as Leonardo, paleoartists no longer had to guess what hadrosaur skin looked like. Now they mostly knew.

Why just "mostly"? Because fossils are like black-and-white photocopies of a photograph or a painting. They show you only shapes and textures. They don't show you colors. For a long time, scientists didn't think they would ever know for sure what colors dinosaurs had been. That's because animal colors are sometimes determined by melanosomes. These are tiny sacs in cells that contain pigment, or color. They are made mostly of protein, and protein doesn't normally stick around after an animal dies. But in 2010, researchers found a small fossilized theropod, complete with its tail—feathers and all. Inside the tail feathers they found remnants of melanosomes that make the colors orange and brown. And from these, the researchers concluded that this dinosaur, *Sinosauropteryx*, had an orange and brown-striped tail.

So far, white, black, ginger, brown, and even a black color with a rainbow-like shimmer (called iridescent) have been found in the feathers of a number of different dinosaur species.

SINOSAUROPTERYX'S STRIPED TAIL

Still missing are melanosomes that would tell scientists the colors of dinosaur skin. They still have to guess at those things based on the colors of other, modern-day animals that also camouflage themselves for safety, like elephants and small lizards. For the time being, what we know about dinosaur colors is all about the feathers.

The Feather Record

It's kind of amazing that we know about feathered dinosaurs at all. *Sinosauropteryx* had a lot to do with it. A whole bunch of these creatures and some other small theropods were found—

many of them complete or near complete—in a large swath of exposed rocks across the countryside in China in the 1990s. Incredibly, they had been fossilized with their feathers. Before they were found, scientists had only guessed that some dinosaurs had had feathers—they hadn't found any proof.

The animal fossils they dug up proved that several different kinds of dinosaurs had feathers: oviraptorosaurs, dromaeosaurids, troodontids, and more primitive theropods like compsognathids. The compsognathids had a thick coating of short feathers all over their bodies. Some of the other specimens had feathered head crests or long feathers sprouting out of their hands, arms, and tails. All over their faces they had a layer of fuzz. The short feathers and fuzz probably helped to insulate the dinosaurs and keep them warm. The longer feathers may have helped with gliding or flying. They may also have been used for mating rituals. This one large cache of dinosaurs helped answer, all at once, a giant question about dinosaurs that had been plaguing paleontologists for years.

Other, smaller finds had big results for our understanding, too. A well-preserved *Archaeopteryx* specimen found in Germany

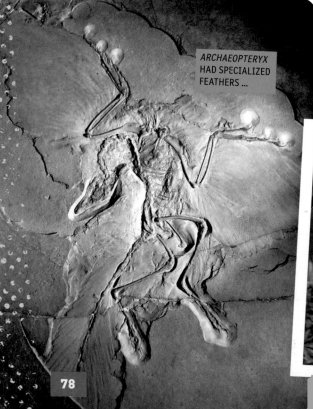

ARCHAEOPTERYX HAD SPECIALIZED FEATHERS ...

... THAT MAY HAVE MEANT IT COULD FLY.

allowed scientists to prove that this bird relative had not only wings but also specialized, complex feathers. These feathers weren't just fuzz to keep the animals warm. With long shafts down their centers, and barbs sticking out from either side of the feather in a V-shaped pattern, they had more in common with flight feathers.

Other fossils have shown the feathers, and their potential uses, of a whole range of dinosaurs. Some tyrannosaurs had feathery filaments all over their bodies. Some ornithomimosaurs had fuzz, plus some long feathers on their arms. *Velociraptor* specimens haven't turned up with their actual feathers or feather impressions, but scientists have found quill knobs in their arm bones, which would have anchored feathers to their bodies—this is another way to show that dinosaurs had feathers, even when you can't find the feathers themselves. There are some scientists who think that *all* dinosaurs may have sported feathers of one kind or another.

WE KNOW *VELOCIRAPTOR* HAD FEATHERS BECAUSE OF QUILL KNOBS.

Tracking Dinosaurs

Fossilized bits and pieces of themselves aren't the only discoverable traces dinosaurs left behind. Think about how you make a trail with your footprints as you walk in snow, wet sand, or mud. That's how dinosaurs left tracks across the surface of our planet. These tracks, made from what are called trace fossils, may not look like anything more than funny-shaped holes in the ground. But they are important records of how dinosaurs spent their time on Earth.

FEATHERS MAY HAVE INSULATED *ARCHAEORNITHOMIMUS* FROM THE COLD.

EVOLUTION OF DINOSAUR FEATHERS

WE KNOW SOME DINOSAURS EVOLVED into birds that could fly. But long before then, their primitive ancestors had some kind of feathers covering their bodies. Scientists are certain the earliest fluffy feathers developed right from dinosaur scales!

SIMPLE DOWNY FEATHERS—for warmth. *(Yutyrannus)*

UNBRANCHED BARBS—even fluffier, the next step in feather evolution. *(Sinosauropteryx)*

PLANAR FEATHERS— flat, with a quill down the center. These may have evolved even before gliding and flight were possible. *(Archaeopteryx)*

PLANAR FEATHER FROM *ARCHAEOPTERYX*

ASYMMETRICAL FLIGHT FEATHERS—fatter on one side of the quill, skinnier on the other to get up into the air. These feathers could possibly indicate dinosaur flight. *(Microraptor)*

HOW A TRACE FOSSIL IS MADE

1. Dinosaurs step on the soft ground and leave footprints.
2. Those footprints dry in the sun and become hardened.
3. The footprints fill up with dirt, mud, sand, and sediment, which also harden.
4. Over time, the sediment inside the footprints erodes, exposing the footprints.

PARALITITAN MAKING TRACE FOSSILS IN A SWAMP

One of the most important things tracks can reveal is where dinosaurs lived. Early paleontologists believed that the largest sauropods were too big to live on land. They thought *Brontosaurus* and other giant plant-eaters must have lived in water, where they could float around as though weightless. But this theory was shown to be incorrect when scientists found sauropod footprints on land—proof that sauropods didn't actually spend their lives swimming in rivers or oceans. Explorer Steve Brusatte and his team's discovery of sauropod tracks on Scotland's Isle of Skye helped refine this knowledge. Those tracks showed that sauropods from the middle Jurassic actually lived very close to the coast and probably even waded in shallow water. So they weren't exactly world-class swimmers, but they did enjoy a little dip now and then.

Other tracks have shown that some dinosaurs lived in places scientists hadn't suspected. For example, footprints of large meat-eating

TRACKWAYS LEFT BEHIND FOR SCIENTISTS TO DISCOVER

dinosaurs found in Australia proved the existence of prehistoric life in what had once been a very cold region of the world. Australia may be a hot desert now, but it was once attached to the frigid region of what eventually became Antarctica—and scientists had thought it was too cold for any dinosaurs to have lived there.

More tracks in Arkansas, U.S.A.—where it was miserably hot and dry during the Cretaceous—show that, surprisingly, some theropods once lived there, too. And where there were theropods, there must also have been other animals for them to eat, including other dinosaurs. These particular tracks also showed that the species of theropod that made them, called *Acrocanthosaurus*, walked with its toes turned inward—also known as pigeon-toed. Once studied further, this knowledge will give more information about the specific ways that *Acrocanthosaurus* walked and ran.

In the country now known as Yemen in the Middle East, 150-million-year-old tracks in the sand were the first evidence paleontologists found of really big ornithopods existing in the late Jurassic. Until this find, most scientists believed that beefy ornithopods didn't evolve until the Cretaceous. This changed the way they began to look at dinosaur evolution.

Countless other tracks all over the world have taught scientists so many other things—both big and small—about the dinosaurs that once ruled our planet. We've learned that some dinosaurs moved around in herds and that others hunted in packs. By measuring tracks for their depth and stride length—that is, how far apart each footprint was from the ones behind and ahead of it—scientists have figured out how fast dinosaurs could run. Preserved tracks have also helped us learn that some dinosaurs lifted their tails as they walked instead of dragging them on the ground. We've learned how dinosaurs tracked their prey, and what they were following. We've learned that some dinosaurs protected their young by placing them in the center of their herd as they moved. We've learned that some dinosaurs had webbed feet, meaning that they were adapted to living in water. And we've even learned that some dinosaurs may have been migratory, moving from place to place with the seasons, or as food scarcity made it necessary.

Sometimes, though, dinosaur tracks create a mystery instead of solving one. Several sets of tracks in the United States, Korea, and Portugal show just the handprints of some unidentified species of dinosaur. This led scientists to wonder: How did *that* happen? Were the dinosaurs wading in the water, using their front feet to pull them along the river bottom? That mystery still remains ... mysterious.

DIPLODOCUS AND *ALLOSAURUS* MADE THESE PRINTS IN GERMANY.

DIG IN

ONE QUESTION ON THE MINDS of paleontologists when they find a new species of dinosaur is: Was it a carnivore, an herbivore, or an omnivore? Teeth give them important clues about the answer.

Sharp teeth helped meat-eaters rip up their food.

A PACK OF *DEINONYCHUS* FIGHTING OVER AND FEEDING ON THEIR PREY.

Create your own carnivore chompers:

A STAPLE REMOVER

COTTON BALLS

Using the staple remover, tear into a cotton ball. (Be sure to keep your fingers out of the way!) Notice how the sharp edges make short work of this delicate piece of "meat"?

Blunt teeth helped
plant-eaters grind up
leaves, twigs,
and cones.

Create your own herbivore chompers:

TWO FLAT
ROCKS

LEAVES
AND TWIGS

Place a leaf or a twig between two rocks
and grind them together. How does this
motion work to make a pulp out of the
plant matter? Do some motions work better than others to break the leaves and
twigs down?

CHAPTER 4

AFTER THE DINOSAURS

A DEVASTATING TIDAL WAVE RUSHES TOWARD LAND AFTER THE METEOR HITS EARTH.

THIS IS WHERE SOME OF THE LAST DINOSAURS ROAMED EARTH.

Standing in this spot, surrounded by the preserved remains of horned dinosaurs, sauropods, duck-billed dinosaurs, and tyrannosaurs, I'm in the middle of the world's best record of what came after the end.

STEVE BRUSATTE

There's an extinction layer here in New Mexico, U.S.A., that includes large amounts of sandstone. This rock was dumped here by big rivers during a time of massive environmental change about 66 million years ago, around the time the Chicxulub asteroid hit hundreds of miles away in what is now Mexico. It's the world's best record of what came after the end-Cretaceous extinction event. And it's one of the only places in the world where you can see how profound the change was—that the planet was dominated by dinosaurs, and then the dinosaurs were just gone, and what remained were new animals that set the stage for how things are today.

What's striking for me is how abrupt the change was, how the world reshaped itself so dramatically in such a short time. We find dinosaur bones everywhere in the Cretaceous rocks, but when we cross into the Paleocene rocks, there are no dinosaurs. There are mammal jaws and teeth everywhere.

What's so important about knowing about this, and seeing it, is that this was one of the biggest turning points in Earth's history. The world drastically changed due to a catastrophe that caused incredible environmental changes that led to extinction. Yes, that extinction happened because a huge asteroid the size of Mount Everest crashed into the planet, which happens only once every half a billion years or so.

After the asteroid hit, there were wildfires, tsunamis, and earthquakes all within the first couple days. Then there were longer-term effects: nuclear winter and global warming. The animals that survived had to put up with a whole lot of nasty stuff. Most of the mammals died, dinosaurs like tyrannosaurs and duckbills died, and only the high-flying birds that could eat seeds survived. We come from that legacy. We probably wouldn't be here if the dinosaurs hadn't died. Without that asteroid, dinosaurs would probably still be around, and mammals would still be living in the shadows.

NEW MEXICO HAS THE WORLD'S BEST RECORD OF WHAT CAME AFTER THE END-CRETACEOUS EXTINCTION EVENT.

WITHOUT THAT ASTEROID, DINOSAURS WOULD PROBABLY STILL BE AROUND.

STEVE ON-SITE IN NEW MEXICO WITH COLLEAGUE TOM WILLIAMSON

SOMETHING BIG HAPPENED ON PLANET EARTH 66 MILLION YEARS AGO.

Something so big that it created a mass extinction. Eighty percent of everything that was alive at the time died, including animals that were just roaming around, doing whatever they did any old day of the week.

The End (but Not Quite)

This mysterious event killed some mammals. It killed marine reptiles. It killed the pterosaurs and tons of plankton and invertebrates living in the oceans. And it killed all the dinosaurs, except for some birds.

Scientists have long argued about what this big thing could have been. They've debated whether it happened all on its own. Or whether it happened in conjunction with, or at the same time as, some other big and small things. Over time they've come to agree on at least one detail. The big thing was an impact that came from outer space. In other words, it was an asteroid or, possibly, a comet.

This asteroid was about six miles (9.7 km) across. As it entered our atmosphere, it was traveling at a speed of 40,000 miles an hour (64,374 km/h)—that's 52 times the speed of sound. It hit Earth—actually, it hit water, since, in the late Cretaceous, the area of impact was completely underneath what's now the Gulf of Mexico—on what's now Mexico's Yucatán Peninsula. When it hit, it exploded with the same force that trillions of tons of TNT all set off at the same time would create. That's several million times stronger than the force of any bomb humans have ever made. When it hit, the asteroid's force was so strong it made a bowl-shaped hole—what we now know as Chicxulub crater—that was 12 miles (19.3 km) deep and 115 miles (185 km) across. The impact was so strong that it

AN ARTIST'S REPRESENTATION OF THE MOUNT EVEREST–SIZE ASTEROID STRIKING THE YUCATÁN PENINSULA

caused the earth to push back upward, creating a ring of mountains inside the crater, just minutes after the asteroid landed.

How do scientists know all this? They confirmed it when they found the crater.

The truth is, they were looking for it. Scientists had suspected for a long time that an asteroid could have caused the K–Pg extinction (that's what scientists call the Cretaceous–Paleogene extinction). They were working off of a really good clue. This was the presence of an element called iridium in the layer of earth that marks the end of the Cretaceous and the beginning of the Paleogene—the same layer where Cretaceous fossils suddenly disappear. Iridium usually isn't found on Earth. It comes from space and is left behind in the ground when asteroids hit.

In 1991, scientists found the Chicxulub crater. It was half in the water, in the Gulf of Mexico, and half on land, on the Yucatán Peninsula. They conducted tests and studies. Recently, they started drilling deep into the crater in search of more clues. They've worked out a pretty good picture of what they think happened 66 million years ago.

The asteroid hit. From there, things went up in flames—literally. For many miles around the

THE CRATER LEFT BEHIND BY THE ASTEROID WAS 112 MILES (180 KM) WIDE.

MEASURING THE FORCE OF THE CHICXULUB ASTEROID

IT HAPPENED 66 MILLION YEARS AGO. So how did scientists figure out how fast the asteroid in Mexico hit Earth? It all has to do with the crater that asteroid left behind, and what scientists found inside it. Drilling 4,380 feet (1,335 m) underneath the floor of the Gulf of Mexico, scientists were able to dig out core samples from the ring of mountains inside the crater. These samples are made of rock, but they don't look like rock you'll find anywhere else in the world. They're composite, made up of different types and colors of rock. The most important type in this instance is granite. That's because granite is usually buried many miles below our planet's surface, in Earth's midcrust. Finding granite allowed scientists to use computers to estimate what speed the meteor had to be moving in order to bring this rock so much closer to Earth's surface.

CHICXULUB CORE SAMPLE

impact site, rock was turned to vapor. Anything within 625 miles (1,005 km) of the impact caught fire. A huge tsunami—or tidal wave—1,000 feet (305 m) high moved across the gulf and rolled over the coasts of both North and South America. In fact, evidence of this tsunami has been found thousands of miles away from Chicxulub, in Montana, U.S.A. Even farther away, in Antarctica, almost everything living in the water died. Massive earthquakes started rumbling. Scientists estimate that these were as strong as every single earthquake of the last 160 years happening at the same time. All the burning debris that was shot into the air when the asteroid hit fell back to Earth.

And all that happened in just the first 10 minutes after impact.

Winds as fast as 600 miles an hour (966 km/h) whipped across the land. Toxic levels of carbon dioxide, carbon monoxide, and methane were released into the air. The ozone layer was destroyed, and the sky turned as dark as night from all the ash and other debris clogging the atmosphere. It got lighter, eventually. But for a few years, Earth was shrouded in darkness.

Over time, this meant that plants weren't exposed to sunlight, so they could not grow. Temperatures plummeted. Some of this killed dinosaurs right away. Some of it killed them slowly over time.

But some scientists wonder, could another small or big thing have helped to kill the dinosaurs? There's evidence that between 2 and 50 million years before Chicxulub, some dinosaurs were already going extinct, such as different species of ceratopsians and hadrosaurs. A few scientists think this means dinosaurs were already well on their way to dying off. Did diseases like malaria have anything to do with it? At least one study shows

MOLTEN ROCK PELTING EARTH AFTER THE ASTEROID HIT

VOLCANIC ERUPTIONS MADE THE AIR TOXIC TO BREATHE AND SHROUDED EARTH IN DARKNESS FOR A FEW YEARS.

that biting midges 100 million years ago carried this sometimes fatal disease and could have passed it on to dinosaurs. Or maybe habitat change made life harder for dinosaurs. This started happening as ocean levels went down in the late Cretaceous, creating more land and less sea.

Even further back, a few million years before Chicxulub, huge volcanic eruptions ravaged what is now India. And around the same time as the asteroid impact, there were also volcanoes going off all over the Pacific Ocean. Some scientists think this helped bring about the end of the dinosaurs. Erupting volcanoes can spew hot lava and ash into the atmosphere, creating global warming. They also pump out lethal amounts of the heavy metal mercury and cause acid rain. These things may have made dinosaurs, along with plants and other animals, unhealthy and unable to survive Chicxulub.

Life in the Cenozoic Era

All across the surface of our planet, millions of animals were dead. Some of them just rotted away right there on the ground where they lay, dissolved by chemicals in the soil. But some of them were quickly covered up by debris from the Chicxulub impact, by ash that spewed out of volcanoes, and by dirt and sand blown around by the winds. Animals that died in the water sank to the bottom of the ocean or riverbeds, where mud and sediment covered them. And sometimes, the conditions were just right for their bones and hard bits to turn into fossils. The bigger and heavier the bones, the more likely they were to fossilize.

Deep underground, fossils were forming. Meanwhile, above ground, new life was springing up all over the place. And all sorts of other amazing things were happening. For instance, the continents continued pulling apart.

HOW DID BIRDS SURVIVE THE EXTINCTION?

THOUSANDS OF DINOSAUR SPECIES were wiped out in the K–Pg extinction. But a few species of birds survived. Fossils show that there may have been ancestors of ducks, loons, pelicans, emus, and even parrots living in the Cretaceous before the extinction. How did they survive?

New research suggests that size had everything to do with it. Many of the bird-line dinosaurs had been evolving into smaller and smaller animals for a while. This happened in conjunction with becoming better fliers. Since birds were so small, they could adapt better to the changed conditions after the Chicxulub asteroid. Benefiting from their mobility, they could also find better habitats. Additionally, small animals can do a better job of hiding from larger, hungry animals.

Another theory is that bird survival had everything to do with their beaks. Where other dinosaurs needed to eat meat or fish or plants—which were in scarce supply after the asteroid hit—bird beaks were well suited to eating seeds. Seeds can survive in the soil for years, providing a ready food supply when no plants can grow. Beaks still serve modern birds very well. By some estimates, there are 10,000 bird species alive on Earth!

BIRDS WERE THE ONLY DINOS TO SURVIVE THE EXTINCTION.

THIS *ARCHOSAURUS* FOSSIL IS NO LONGER BONE—IT'S ROCK.

TURNING TO STONE

HERE'S HOW BONE TURNS INTO FOSSIL:

1. The layers of dirt covering a dinosaur are pressed together and turn into sedimentary rock.
2. Inside that rock, water from the ground that's filled with minerals starts to seep into the dinosaur's bones and dissolve the tissue.
3. Meanwhile, the minerals in the water replace the materials that make up the bones, filling in all the spaces where other materials have dissolved.
4. Millions of years later, voilà, fossils!

You would have been able to look at a map of the world by 50 million years ago and feel almost at home. But the continents still had funny shapes and weren't yet in exactly the places we're used to seeing them.

The breakup of the continents was good news for diversity. Each continent developed its own climate, which helped different species of plants and animals evolve. Think about how you see kangaroos only in Australia and polar bears only in the Arctic. They are adapted to their particular environments.

Overall, though, the temperatures fluctuated a lot on Earth during the years leading up to humans. First, the Cenozoic era was really hot. Then it got super hot. Then an ice age swept over the North and South Poles. Through it all, animals that hadn't been able to truly thrive during the dinosaur age finally got their time to shine. Different kinds of ray-finned fish filled the oceans. This group included tuna, goldfish, and eels. Insects continued to evolve, including moths, beetles, bees, and wasps. These insects were eaten by the growing numbers and types of birds, the only dinosaurs to survive the K–Pg extinction. Among plants, some of the gymnosperms became less diverse. But new kinds of leafy trees emerged, along with many more kinds of ferns, flowers, and most of all, grasses.

Most dramatic of all, though, was the evolution of mammals. Sure, there were some mammals existing out there before the extinction. But scientists believe that competition for resources from the dinosaurs kept them from really taking off. Once the dinosaurs were gone, the mammals that survived the extinction quickly became bigger, more diverse, and better at adapting to new conditions on the planet. Not all of them survived long enough to live at the same time as humans. Rhino-like, plant-eating *Uintatherium,* with giraffe-like knobs all over its head, never made it into the Quaternary period. Neither did *Andrewsarchus,* a massive, fuzzy meat-eater from Mongolia that resembled a wild boar. Or an early bat called *Icaronycteris.* They joined the dinosaurs in extinction, and some of their bones went into the ground to turn slowly into fossils, giving paleontologists a record of how life changed over time. A record that leads all the way to today.

MAMMAL *UINTATHERIUM* WAS A LOT LIKE A RHINO!

Digging Into the Past

So fossils are buried deep in the ground, covered with millions of years' worth of earth junk. Most of them stay buried, where we'll never, ever see them. But some of them come right up to the surface, where they can be found by humans. How is this possible? It's called uplift, and it happens when the rocky plates that together form the shell of our planet, just beneath the crust, start to shift or even crash together. This movement makes deep-down rock buckle and push upward, creating mountains. But uplift has a secondary effect. Those rocks that are now exposed to the surface of Earth are eroded by sun, rain, and wind. Over time, the rock is worn away enough that fossils become visible.

That's when it's time to cue the fossil hunters!

AMMONITE FOSSILS REVEALED ON MONMOUTH BEACH IN ENGLAND

The Fossil Hunters

People have been finding fossils for thousands of years. But they haven't always known what their treasures were. Perhaps dragon bones? Pieces of monsters from mythological stories?

Some of the old names for fossils show how little people understood about the prehistoric world. Fossilized ammonites were called snakestones, because they showed a curled shape that looked like a napping snake. Gnarly black Jurassic-era oyster fossils were called devil's toenails. Coprolites were called bezoar stones and were thought to have magical powers against poisoning. Fossilized, bullet-shaped cuttlefish ancestors were known as thunderbolts.

Little by little, though, people interested in science began to figure out that fossils weren't just pretty objects made of rocks. They were important records of the past, and of creatures that had lived long, long ago.

IN WILLIAM BUCKLAND'S DAY, AMMONITES WERE "SNAKESTONES" AND OYSTERS WERE "DEVIL'S TOENAILS."

STEVE BRUSATTE

▼

MY COLLEAGUE TOM WILLIAMSON at the New Mexico Museum of Natural History and Science has amassed an incredible collection of fossils over the last 25 years. He has twin boys, Ryan and Taylor, who he's been taking out to the field with him every year since they were about six years old. Now they're in college. Those boys have found some amazing fossils, including the earliest skeleton of a primate.

Anyone can find fossils—that's one of the great things about studying ancient creatures. But it's important to remember that when paleontologists go out and collect, we have permits, and we know what the laws about collecting are. Most discoveries these days are made by farmers or construction workers, and a lot are made by kids out hiking with their parents. How cool is that? But you should always report your discovery when you find a fossil. Don't remove it, because that could destroy it. Leave it where it is, and call the local museum or university and say, "Hey, I found this fossil!" They will be very happy you called.

Many times, we name fossils after the people who found them. Maybe one day that will be you!

The first time scientists really took an interest in fossils was in the late 17th century. That's when an English naturalist named Robert Plot found a massive femur, or thighbone, in a quarry. At first, he thought it belonged to an elephant that had been brought to England during the time of the Romans. Then he changed his mind and decided it must have belonged to a giant human. But guess what? Today we know it belonged to *Megalosaurus*.

Back then, even the most educated people believed Earth was only a few thousand years old. They also thought that fossils belonged to animal species that still existed. But they had a hard time figuring out what animals these fossils could belong to. Many of them didn't look like bones from any species they had ever seen.

Then, a French naturalist named Georges Cuvier had a revelation. Those fossils must have come from animals that had gone extinct. This was a mind-blowing idea at the time. Scientists fought about it for many years. But because of this radical idea, Cuvier became known as the father of paleontology. The word "paleontology" means the study of old things, particularly fossils, and it was coined in the mid-1800s.

That's when fossil hunting really started to take off. In England especially, many impressive fossils were found and discussed in scientific circles. A doctor named Gideon Mantell found a big tooth in West Sussex. He would later call the animal this tooth belonged to *Iguanodon*. Two years after that first find, a geologist named William Buckland announced that a jawbone that had been sitting in a museum belonged to a giant lizard, or *Megalosaurus*. More *Iguanodon* bones were found, then bones from *Hylaeosaurus*. And it became clear that

FOSSIL HUNTING IN NEW MEXICO: STEVE'S COLLEAGUES SARAH SHELLEY AND TOM WILLIAMSON

GIDEON MANTELL'S DRAWINGS OF *IGUANODON* TEETH

these bones did not belong to any animals still existing on Earth. They belonged to a wholly different group of reptiles. In 1841, a paleontologist named Richard Owen proposed the name "dinosaur." It means "fearfully great lizard."

The Bone Wars

The fever for fossils was already running high in England. Then the first *Trachodon*, *Troodon*, and *Deinodon* teeth were found in the United States in the 1850s. This doubled

HYLAEOSAURUS HELPED EARLY FOSSIL-HUNTERS UNDERSTAND DINOSAURS.

MARY ANNING

MARY ANNING WAS BORN just before the turn of the 19th century. Back then, men dominated, well, everything, including the sciences. Across England and Europe, men of science brought their latest research and discoveries to scientific societies to be discussed and debated. No women were allowed.

Mary Anning happened to live in a part of southern coastal England that was chock-full of fossils from the Jurassic period. These were buried in the seaside cliffs of her hometown of Lyme Regis. As the tides and weather eroded those cliffs, incredible fossils were exposed. In 1811, Anning and her brother found an amazing skeleton there: the first discovered ichthyosaur. Over the years, Anning would dig other ichthyosaurs out of the Lyme Regis cliffs, along with the first plesiosaur. This brought the men of science straight to her door. They bought her fossils. They studied them, and then reported their findings to the scientific societies. They almost

SUPER FOSSIL-HUNTER MARY ANNING

never gave Anning credit for her discoveries. Even so, she studied her finds and developed her own theories about what they were.

So why did she go along with it? She needed the money. Anning was born into poverty and remained poor for most of her life. The money the male scientists spent to purchase her fossils—some of which even showed up in museum collections—helped her to eat and also to set up a souvenir shop. There, she sold other, smaller fossils to the tourists who came to town every summer to bask on the beach.

Anning was never famous in her lifetime, although her name was familiar to many of the paleontologists of her time. But almost 200 years after her death, we finally know that she is one of the most accomplished fossil-hunters the world has ever known. She's famous in another way, too. Have you ever heard the tongue twister "She sells seashells by the seashore"? That was written about Mary Anning!

COPE AND MARSH

HERE ARE JUST A FEW of the more than 120 now-famous dinosaurs Cope and Marsh described and named:

COPE

ALLOSAURUS

TRICERATOPS

DIPLODOCUS

MARSH

BRONTOSAURUS

EDMONTOSAURUS

the number of dinosaur species that had been described so far—now there were six. Then, in 1870, a huge heap of dinosaur fossils was found in Colorado. And paleontologists went completely bananas. This discovery started what was called the Bone Wars, also known as the Great Dinosaur Rush.

For 20 years, two men in particular competed against each other to find new fossils belonging to brand-new dinosaurs. They were the paleontologists Edward Drinker Cope and Othniel Marsh. Cope took teams of bone hunters out into what was still Indian Territory in Wyoming and Colorado. Marsh was the curator of the Peabody Museum of Natural History in New Haven, Connecticut. Both men hired other people to do the dirty work of digging for them.

Actually, "dirty" is a good word for some of

the tricks Marsh used to make sure all the best fossils came to his museum. And Cope used those tricks, too. The two men said mean things about each other in the newspapers. They spied on each other's digs. They blew up each other's dig sites with dynamite. And they stole each other's fossils. But between the two of them (and with help from their hardworking crews), they found and named more than 120 new dinosaurs. The men may not have been the nicest or the most ethical people, but they certainly made huge contributions to science! This dinosaur fever didn't come to an end when Cope and Marsh gave up competing with each other to find fossils. (They'd actually competed so hard, and for so long, that they both ran out of money.) Plenty of other people searched for dinosaur bones in the 19th and 20th centuries, too. And every find helped further our understanding of what dinosaurs were, how they lived, and how they evolved.

All over the world, dinosaurs were being dug up, including in South America, Germany, and Egypt. Even today, new paleontologists are still making discoveries. All told, more than 1,000 different species of dinosaurs have been identified so far. Scientists think that number represents a small fraction of the dinosaur species that lived on Earth for 165 million years. Imagine how many more dinosaurs must be out there (or rather, *down* there), waiting to be discovered!

A Tour of the World's Boneyards

Finding one dinosaur—or even one part of a dinosaur—is totally awesome. Finding many dinosaurs is mind-blowing. More than that, a huge trove of fossils can give researchers enough material to study for years at a time.

Boneyards give paleontologists just this kind of material. These are natural graveyards filled with fossils. The kinds of fossils that are found in one have to do with what animals once lived nearby, of course. And how good the conditions were for preserving their remains.

North America has some famous and important boneyards. One of these is Dinosaur National Monument. It is chock-full of Jurassic-period fossils. It's made up of 600,000 square miles (1,553,993 sq km) of sedimentary rock in Colorado and Utah, and it's the site of the Morrison Formation, where Cope and Marsh made most of their discoveries during the Bone Wars.

Barnum Brown, who discovered the first

BRONTOSAURUS SKELETON ON DISPLAY AT YALE UNIVERSITY'S PEABODY MUSEUM

T. rex, which he found in Montana, also excavated Howe Quarry in Wyoming, where he found *Diplodocus* bones and bunches of teeth from different kinds of theropods. But the finds didn't end there. More recently, a team of paleontologists have found what they think is a whole new species of sauropod in Howe Quarry. They've named it *Kaatedocus siberi.* Nearby, in the Hell Creek Formation in Montana, so many different kinds of Cretaceous dinosaurs have been found that it's hard to keep count! Ankylosaurs, pachycephalosaurs, ceratopsians, hadrosaurs, tyrannosaurs, ornithomimosaurs—and the list goes on.

Some of the oldest, and some of the biggest, dinosaur fossils come from South America. Argentina is one of the southernmost countries in South America. Its tip reaches almost all the way to Antarctica. It is the site of two super-important boneyards. One of these is the Ischigualasto Formation, a desert area that lies up in cliffs that are 4,300 feet (1,310 m) high. This is a dry and barren region, and its climate has helped preserve much of what there is to know about the Triassic dinosaurs and mammals buried inside its rocks. Ischigualasto has been studied since about 1930, with more dinosaur species discovered there than you can count—because new ones are still being found. Of all the dinosaurs that lived in Ischigualasto, *Eoraptor* might have been its most famous resident.

Auca Mahuevo, located a little bit south of Ischigualasto, is famous for Cretaceous dinosaurs. More specifically, eggs of the giant sauropod *Saltasaurus*. In 1997, Lowell Dingus and his team of paleontologists found layers of eggs and

PATAGOTITAN WAS FOUND HERE, IN ARGENTINA.

THE GERMAN QUARRY WHERE THE FIRST *ARCHAEOPTERYX* FOSSIL WAS FOUND

eggshells buried here. Some of them were still lying arranged in clutches in their nests, just the way their mothers must have laid them millions of years ago. Many of them contained fossilized embryos. The number of eggs and egg remains found here is so impressive that scientists have taken to calling Auca Mahuevo an egg bed instead of a bone bed or boneyard. This massive sauropod nesting site is just a few hours south of another important place for sauropods: Argentina's Mendoza Province, where in 2014 a rancher stumbled on the remains of the *Patagotitan mayorum,* the biggest of all the dinosaurs ever found.

Hop across the Atlantic Ocean to southern Germany. Here in a quarry in the town of Solnhofen, the first ever *Archaeopteryx* fossil was found in 1861. This amazing fossil actually included material from a feather. This find was the first of several

PALEONTOLOGISTS AT WORK IN RUKWA RIFT BASIN

that led to the realization that *Archaeopteryx* was a transitional species between dinosaurs that couldn't fly and dinosaurs that could fly. Since then, fossils from more than 10 other *Archaeopteryx* have been found in the same rock formation. Something about this region must have appealed to animals that could fly, because many well-preserved fossils of Jurassic pterosaurs were also found there.

The first ever fossilized dinosaurs excavated in Africa came from Tanzania. The country's Tendaguru Beds were excavated starting in 1906, and, strangely, a lot of the fossils found there were similar to fossils found in the western part of the United States. *Brachiosaurus* was kind of like *Giraffatitan* from Tendaguru, and *Stegosaurus* was like Tendaguru's *Kentrosaurus.* In 2014, a team of paleontologists from Ohio, U.S.A., found a new

100-million-year-old titanosaur to the west of Tendaguru, at a site called the Rukwa Rift Basin. This dino is called *Rukwatitan bisepultus*. It just goes to show that boneyards can keep giving up fossils, even after they've already been excavated.

There are many other superamazing boneyards across the world, including some in other parts of Europe, and in Egypt and Australia. But two others stand out from the rest. One of these is in Liaoning, in northern China. This is one of the newest of the boneyards that have been discovered so far. In this spot around 125 million years ago, in the early Cretaceous, volcanoes killed off huge numbers of dinosaurs. Many farmers in the region have found many new kinds of dinosaurs—so far, about 60 of them. It's because of some of these discoveries that we now know that many of the dinosaurs we used to think had scales actually had feathers. And because these dinosaurs have been so well preserved, they still have melanosomes in their feathers. These are the dinosaurs that have helped scientists figure out what colors some dinosaurs may have been. *Sinosauropteryx* is from Liaoning. So are the other feathered dinosaurs *Anchiornis huxleyi*, *Epidexipteryx,* and the remarkable mule-size *Zhenyuanlong suni*.

And last but not least, there's Mount Kirkpatrick in Antarctica. Millions of years ago, Antarctica was not nearly as freezing cold and snow covered as it is now. And it turns out, many dinosaurs once lived there. Mount Kirkpatrick is where many have been found. That's because it's one of the few places on the continent where

INCISIVOSAURUS GAUTHIERI SKULL FOUND IN LIAONING

fossils aren't buried under many deep layers of ice. In 1991, a team of paleontologists led by William Hammer went to Antarctica to dig for fossils. It wasn't easy to get to them. The team had to use jackhammers to break through the ice. They couldn't study the fossils on-site, so they had to break off big blocks of rock and send them back to their lab in Illinois, U.S.A.

When they were finally able to clean up those rocks and study them, they knew what they had found months earlier in the ice: the first dinosaur from Antarctica to ever be named. This was a new meat-eating species they called *Cryolophosaurus*. Since then, the team has found many more of these dinosaurs on Mount Kirkpatrick, as well as some large sauropods that resemble *Diplodocus,* and an unnamed 200-million-year-old ornithischian. That leads scientists to wonder: Was there anywhere on our planet that dinosaurs did not roam? More and more, it's looking like the answer to that question is no!

CRYOLOPHOSAURUS

EVIDENCE OF DINOSAURS HAS BEEN FOUND ALL OVER THE WORLD!

WHERE WILL THE NEXT FOSSILS BE DISCOVERED?

ALBERTA, CANADA Big find: a new ceratopsian species later named *Regaliceratops*

HELL CREEK, MONTANA, U.S.A.
Big finds: several *Tyrannosaurus rex* specimens, *Triceratops,* and many other late Cretaceous dinosaurs

DINOSAUR NATIONAL MONUMENT, UTAH, U.S.A.
Big finds: several large plant-eaters, including *Apatosaurus* and *Barosaurus,* and meat-eaters such as *Allosaurus*

FAITH, SOUTH DAKOTA, U.S.A.
Big find: Sue the *T. rex*

NORTH AMERICA

ARKANSAS, U.S.A.
Big find: tracks from a thero-pod called *Acrocanthosaurus*

PALUXY RIVER, TEXAS, U.S.A. Big finds: trackways showing an encounter between a large plant-eater and a large meat-eater in the early Cretaceous

ATLANTIC OCEAN

PACIFIC OCEAN

ISCHIGUALASTO, ARGENTINA
Big finds: two of the oldest dinosaurs known—the meat-eaters *Eoraptor* and *Herrerasaurus*

SOUTH AMERICA

MENDOZA PROVINCE, ARGENTINA
Big find: the world's largest titanosaur, *Patagotitan mayorum*

PLAZA HUINCUL, ARGENTINA
Big finds: some of the largest meat-eating and plant-eating dinosaurs in the world, including *Argentinosaurus, Giganotosaurus,* and *Mapusaurus,* as well as many other species

AUCA MAHUEVO, ARGENTINA
Big find: a dinosaur nesting site with thousands of eggs, some of them unhatched

ISLE OF SKYE, SCOTLAND, U.K.
Big find: sauropod tracks from the middle Jurassic

BERNISSART, BELGIUM
Big finds: many well-preserved *Iguanodon* dinosaurs

THE GOBI, MONGOLIA
Big finds: some of the best-preserved dinosaur skeletons, including the fighting *Velociraptor* and *Protoceratops*

SOLNHOFEN, GERMANY
Big finds: *Compsognathus*, *Archaeopteryx*, and many late Jurassic plants, fish, and other animals

EUROPE

ASIA

LIAONING, CHINA Big find: preserved fossils of many early Cretaceous animals, including feathered dinosaurs such as *Mei* and *Microraptor*

MADAR, YEMEN Big find:
researchers discover ornithopod tracks

SHANDONG PENINSULA, CHINA
Big find: one of the largest hadrosaurs, *Shantungosaurus*

AFRICA

PACIFIC OCEAN

THE SAHARA, NIGER Big finds: *Suchomimus*, *Deltadromeus*, and other Cretaceous dinosaurs

TENDAGURU, TANZANIA
Big finds: *Brachiosaurus*, *Allosaurus*, *Kentrosaurus*, *Barosaurus*, *Ceratosaurus*, and others

LARK QUARRY, AUSTRALIA
Big finds: thousands of dinosaur footprints and fossils of *Diamantinasaurus* and *Wintonotitan*

AUSTRALIA

INDIAN OCEAN

MOUNT KIRKPATRICK, ANTARCTICA
Big find: a new meat-eating species called *Cryolophosaurus*

ANTARCTICA

101

SIFTING
THE FINDS

DIGGING OUT
FOSSILS

Fossil Science

The basics of finding fossils have been consistent for 200 years. A paleontologist takes a team of diggers someplace he or she thinks they are likely to find dinosaur fossils. A boneyard that's already been excavated, for example. Or a site where a regular person just happened to find a fossil. Or maybe the team starts hunting in a place that has rock that's good for fossil hunting. This usually means sandstone or other sedimentary rock. Sedimentary rock is formed when layers of dirt and sand are piled on top of each other. The bones turn to stone over millions of years, as do any bones that have been trapped inside them. When a paleontologist finds what might be the right spot, the team starts digging.

This process is slow and difficult. And it has to be done by hand. Paleontologists want to make sure they don't destroy any fossils they're trying to dig up. They might have to blast through rock or ice using jackhammers,

as Dr. Hammer did in Antarctica. But mostly they use tools like chisels, hammers, and saws—and even sharp dental tools—to free bones from the rock, especially when they get close to them. They also use soft brushes to dust off the fossils so they can see them better as they dig them out. And they paint soft glue over fossils to keep them from falling apart.

Before removing anything from a dig site, paleontologists make a map of what they've found. They take photographs and draw diagrams that show precisely where every bone lies. This way, scientists have a record of the fossil site to study, to figure out which bones belong together. This is especially important when lots of fossils are found at a site. As they lie in the ground throughout the passing millennia, they often become jumbled. It can be hard to sort them all out!

Dr. Hammer in Antarctica had to remove huge chunks of rock from the earth. He sent them back to the lab with the fossils still completely encased inside. But often, paleontologists can dig out bones right at the fossil site. Small bones may be fragile, but they are easily wrapped up and protected for the journey back to the lab. Bigger bones are more of a challenge. Paleontologists have to pack these up in plaster so they stay in one piece as they travel. Barnum Brown is credited with inventing this method in the 19th century, and scientists have been using it ever since. They dip strips of burlap in wet plaster. Then they tightly wrap these strips around each bone, creating a giant mummy. If you've ever made a papier-mâché sculpture, you've worked like a paleontologist out in the field. Each bone is labeled with numbers and letters that will help scientists identify it later. Everything is packed in crates and sent off.

These techniques have been used since the early days of fossil hunting and are still used today. But new technologies now help paleontologists figure out where to dig for dinosaur bones and other remains of long-extinct animals. One such technology is LiDAR. This stands for light detection and ranging. LiDAR is used by scientists who want to make accurate 3-D maps of items they can't really get a good look at on their own—like the shape of the ocean's bottom, the coastline, or the lay of the land under a deep forest canopy. LiDAR pulses thousands of points of laser light at an area and measures how far each of those points travels, which lets you see surfaces in great detail. LiDAR helped scientists at the Dinosaur National Monument create a

map of the huge, complicated wall of bones that's on display there, for example.

Drones are another new tool helping paleontologists in their work. These are remote-controlled robots that can be outfitted with little cameras. They can fly low over places that are too remote or treacherous to be reached on foot. They're also used at sporting events to show you up-close plays by your favorite athletes. Drones help paleontologists find trace fossils, like dinosaur footprints, that might be hiding in plain sight. In fact, drones helped scientists in western Australia find and map thousands of 130-million-year-old theropod and sauropod tracks along dangerous pieces of rocky coastline. Eventually, studying the footage collected by drones will allow the scientists to better understand the way these dinosaurs traveled.

DRONES HELP PALEONTOLOGISTS SEE HARD-TO-REACH PLACES.

PALEONTOLOGIST DARLA ZELENITSKY PREPARING AN ORNITHOMIMID BONE SPECIMEN IN THE GOBI

THE DINO LAB AT PHILADELPHIA'S ACADEMY OF NATURAL SCIENCES

Back at the Lab

Once the fossils have made their way back to the lab, a whole other type of work begins—figuring out which era they actually belong to. Paleontologists usually have at least a rough idea. They base it on the level—and, therefore, the age—of sediment they dug the fossils out of. This is called stratigraphy.

The fossils also have to be identified—do they belong to a species that's already known to science? Or have paleontologists really lucked out and discovered a whole new kind of dinosaur? So after scientists have cleaned their fossil finds up by taking them out of their plaster cases and removing any last bits of rock, they take pictures. Not just any pictures, but 3-D images that get stored in computers. Museums try to record every dinosaur bone in their collections this way, too. These images let scientists compare new finds to old finds, to see what's the same and what might be different. They can also go back into the museum's collections and read the field notes that other paleontologists have made about their finds. In this way, they start to get a picture of what their dinosaur might have looked and acted like.

These 3-D images also let scientists do another supercool thing, called computer modeling. Entering the pictures of the dinosaur's bones, along with other information like how much the bones weigh, scientists can use a computer program to work out important details. How would these bones have fit together? How

3-D SCAN OF A *TRICERATOPS* SKULL

SCIENTISTS MADE THIS ROBOTIC DINO SKELETON WITH A 3-D PRINTER.

would this dinosaur have stood and walked—and how fast could it move? How would it have been able to swing or rotate its head and tail? How would its muscles have fit over its bones? Did its jaws move only up and down, or could they move side to side, too? Thanks to computer modeling, scientists have changed some of their ideas about these prehistoric animals—changes that now show up in the way dinosaurs are exhibited in museums.

Exhibiting dinosaurs presents its own challenges. Paleontologists rarely find a complete skeleton. They have to make replacement bones to fill in what's missing. Also, ancient fossils are extremely delicate and sometimes very heavy. So it's rare for a real fossil to make it out to a museum's exhibit hall. Once scientists know how a skeleton fits together, model makers make casts of the actual bones in order to make lightweight replicas of the skeleton. That's what you're usually looking at in a prehistoric museum exhibit.

THE REAL SKULL (LEFT) AND THE MAN-MADE RE-CREATION (RIGHT)

Does this make you wish that you could touch and study real live dinosaur bones, instead of just viewing replicas from a distance? If so, it's possible that you have the makings of the next great paleontologist! Just think of all the dinosaurs still waiting to be discovered and all the techniques—both new and old—that can help you find, study, and understand them. The world might just be one giant dinosaur boneyard.

Don't just sit there—it's time to start digging up those mysteries!

DIG IN

PALEONTOLOGISTS HAVE TO BE well prepared when they look for traces of creatures and plants out in the field. You never know what you might need! Think about what happens on a dig. What kinds of tools might you want to have by your side?

Try putting together your own field kit from items around your home. (Be sure to ask an adult before borrowing any tools!) Then head outside with your paleo-excavation team—including an adult to help with looking in high places—to see what you can find! Remember to leave anything you find right where it is, and if you think you've found a dinosaur, report it to your local museum!

STEVE REVEALING FOSSILIZED TRACKS ON THE ISLE OF SKYE, SCOTLAND

CHINESE PALEONTOLOGISTS EXCAVATING *MAMENCHISAURUS*, IN CHONGQING, CHINA

A PALEONTOLOGIST EXCAVATES A PLEISTOCENE SITE IN SOUTH DAKOTA, U.S.A.

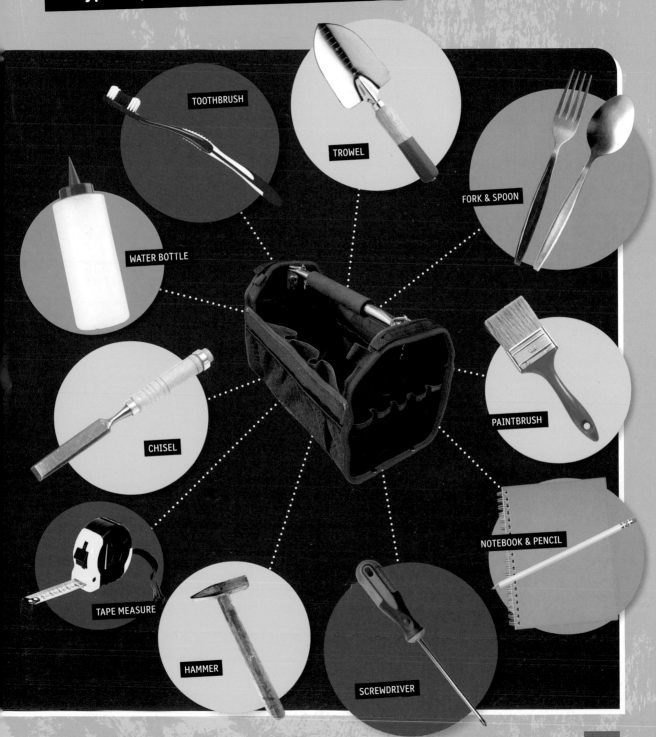

A typical paleontological field kit might include these tools:

TOOTHBRUSH

TROWEL

FORK & SPOON

WATER BOTTLE

CHISEL

PAINTBRUSH

TAPE MEASURE

NOTEBOOK & PENCIL

HAMMER

SCREWDRIVER

PRONUNCIATION GUIDE

Here's how to pronounce some of the prehistoric species in this book.

ABELISAURUS (ay-bel-uh-SORE-us)
ACROCANTHOSAURUS (ACK-row-CAN-tho-SORE-us)
ALBERTONECTES (AL-burr-toe-NEK-tees)
ALIORAMUS (AL-ee-oh-RAY-mus)
ALLOSAURUS (AL-oh-SORE-us)
ALXASAURUS (AWL-shah-SORE-us)
AMPHICOELIAS (AM-feh-SEE-lee-us)
ANCHIORNIS (ANN-kee-OR-niss)
ANDREWSARCHUS (AN-drew-ZARK-us)
APATOSAURUS (uh-PAT-uh-SORE-us)
ARCHAEOPTERYX (ARK-ee-OP-turr-icks)
ARGENTINOSAURUS (ahr-gen-TEEN-oh-SORE-us)
ASKEPTOSAURUS (ah-SKEP-tuh-SORE-us)
BRACHIOSAURUS (BRACK-ee-oh-SORE-us)
BRONTOSAURUS (BRON-tuh-SORE-us)
CAMARASAURUS (KAM-ah-rah-SORE-us)
CARCHARODONTOSAURUS
    (CAR-care-oh-DON-toe-SORE-us)

PSITTACOSAURUS
(SIT-AH-CO-SORE-US)

CARNOTAURUS (KAR-no-TORE-us)
CERATOSAURUS (ser-RAT-uh-SORE-us)
CHAOHUSAURUS (KAY-huh-SORE-us)
COLEPIOCEPHALE (COLE-ep-ee-oh-SEFF-al-ee)
COMPSOGNATHUS (KOMP-sog-NAH-thus or
    komp-SOG-no-thus)
CONFUCIUSORNIS (con-FEW-shuh-SORE-niss)
CRYOLOPHOSAURUS (CRY-oh-LOW-fo-SORE-us)
CTENOCHASMA (kuh-TEN-oh-KAZ-mah)
CYNOGNATHUS (sih-NOG-nuh-thiss)
DEINOCHEIRUS (DINE-oh-KYE-russ)
DEINONYCHUS (die-NON-e-kuss)
DILOPHOSAURUS (die-LOAF-o-SORE-us)
DIMETRODON (die-MET-reh-don)
DIPLOCAULUS (dih-pluh-KAWL-us)
DIPLODOCUS (dih-PLOD-uh-kus)
DREPANOSAURUS (drep-a-nih-SORE-us)
EDMONTOSAURUS (ed-MON-toh-SORE-us)
ELASMOSAURUS (ee-LAZ-muh-SORE-us)
EORAPTOR (EE-oh-RAP-tore)
EOZOSTRODON (ee-uh-ZOS-tra-don)
EPIDEXIPTERYX (EP-ee-DEX-ip-terr-icks)
EUDIMORPHODON (yu-dee-MORE-fih-don)
FALCARIUS (fal-KEH-ree-us)
GALLIMIMUS (GAL-i-MIME-us)
GALLODACTYLUS (gal-ih-DAK-til-us)
GIGANOTOSAURUS (JYE-ga-NO-toe-SORE-us)
GIRAFFATITAN (ji-RAFF-ah-TYE-tan)
GORGOSAURUS (GORE-go-SORE-us)
GOYOCEPHALE (GOH-yo-SEFF-ah-lee)
HYLAEOSAURUS (hie-LEE-oh-SORE-us)
HYPACROSAURUS (hi-PACK-row-SORE-us)
ICARONYCTERIS (IK-ah-ron-IK-ter-iss)
IGUANODON (ig-WAN-oh-don)
ISANOSAURUS (ee-sahn-o-SORE-us)
JURATYRANT (JOO-ra-TYE-rant)
KAATEDOCUS (kaht-uh-DOKE-us)
KENTROSAURUS (KEN-troh-SORE-us)

KUEHNEOSAURUS (KWAIN-ee-o-SORE-us)
MAGNAPAULIA (MAG-nuh-PORE-lee-uh)
MAGYAROSAURUS (MAG-yar-o-SORE-us)
MAIASAURA (MA-ya-SORE-a)
MAJUNGASAURUS (mah-JOONG-ah-SORE-us)
MAMENCHISAURUS (mah-MEHN-chee-SORE-us)
MEGALOSAURUS (MEG-ah-low-SORE-us)
MEGAZOSTRODON (MEG-ah-ZOS-troh-don)
METOPOSAURUS (mee-TOP-oh-SORE-us)
MICRORAPTOR (MY-crow-RAP-tore)
MOSASAURUS (MOW-suh-SORE-us)
MOSCHOPS (maz-KOPS)
NOTHOSAURUS (NAH-thuh-SORE-us)
OVIRAPTOR (OH-vih-RAP-tore)
PACHYCEPHALOSAURUS
    (pack-ih-SEF-ah-low-SORE-us)
PACHYRHINOSAURUS (pack-ee-RINE-oh-SORE-us)
PARASAUROLOPHUS (PAR-ah-saw-RAH-loh-fuss)
PATAGOTITAN (PAT-uh-go-TI-TAN)
PENTACERATOPS (PEN-ta-SER-ah-tops)
PINACOSAURUS (PIN-ah-co-SORE-us)
PLACERIAS (PLAY-sir-EE-us)
PLACODUS (PLAY-kud-us)
PLATEOSAURUS (PLAT-ee-oh-SORE-us)
POSTOSUCHUS (pohs-TOE-suk-us)
PROROTODACTYLUS (pro-ROH-toe-DAK-til-us)
PROTOCERATOPS (PRO-toh-SER-ah-tops)
PSITTACOSAURUS (SIT-ah-co-SORE-us)
PTERODACTYL (TARE-oh-DAK-til)
PTERODACTYLUS (TARE-oh-DAK-til-us)
QIANZHOUSAURUS (chyan-shoo-SORE-us)
QUETZALCOATLUS (KET-sahl-COAT-lus)
RAJASAURUS (rah-jah-SORE-us)
RAPETOSAURUS (RAH-peh-to-SORE-us)
REGALICERATOPS (REG-ah-li-SER-ah-tops)
RUKWATITAN (ROOK-wa-TIE-tan)
SALTASAURUS (SALT-ah-SORE-us)
SALTOPUS (SALT-oh-puss)
SAUROPOSEIDON (SORE-oh-PO-sye-don)
SCLEROMOCHLUS (sklair-AH-muhk-lus)
SHANTUNGOSAURUS (SHAHN-DUNG-oh-SORE-us)
SINOCALLIOPTERYX (SINE-o-CAL-ee-AWP-ter-iks)

SINOSAUROPTERYX (SINE-oh-sore-OP-ter-iks)
SINRAPTOR (sine-RAP-tore)
SPINOSAURUS (SPINE-oh-SORE-us)
STEGOSAURUS (STEG-oh-SORE-us)
STRUTHIOMIMUS (strooth-ee-oh-MY-muss)
STYRACOSAURUS (sty-RACK-oh-SORE-us)
TENONTOSAURUS (ten-ONT-oh-SORE-us)
THERIZINOSAURUS (THERE-ih-ZIN-oh-SORE-us)
TIMURLENGIA (tee-MUR-len-gee-a)
TITANOCERATOPS (tye-TAN-oh-SER-ah-tops)
TRACHODON (TRAK-oh-don)
TRICERATOPS (tri-SERR-uh-tops)
TRIOPTICUS (tri-OP-tih-cus)
TROODON (TRO-oh-don)
TYRANNOSAURUS (tye-RAN-oh-SORE-us)
UGRUNAALUK (oo-GREW-na-luck)
UINTATHERIUM (YU-in-tah-THER-ee-um)
UTAHRAPTOR (YOO-tah-RAP-tore)
VELOCIRAPTOR (veh-LOSS-ih-RAP-tore)
WIEHENVENATOR (vee-HEN-vuh-NAY-tore)
YUTYRANNUS (yoo-tye-RAN-us)
ZHENYUANLONG (ZHEN-yoo-an-LONG)

FOR MORE DINOSAUR READING, CHECK OUT:

Agresta, Jen, and Avery Elizabeth Hurt. *Dino Records: The Most Amazing Prehistoric Creatures Ever to Have Lived on Earth!* National Geographic Kids Books, 2017.

Aronson, Marc, and Adrienne Mayor. *The Griffin and the Dinosaur: How Adrienne Mayor Discovered a Fascinating Link Between Myth and Science.* National Geographic Kids Books, 2014.

Hoena, Blake. *Everything Dinosaurs.* National Geographic Kids Books, 2014.

Lessem, Don. *Ultimate Dinopedia,* 2nd ed. National Geographic Kids Books, 2017.

IMAGE CREDITS

ASP: Alamy Stock Photo; GI: Getty Images; SCI: Science Source; SS: Shutterstock
All illustrations by Franco Tempesta, except as noted:

4 (pickaxe), Stocksnapper/SS; 5 (Triceratops), David Herraez Calzada/SS; 5 (Ankylosaur), leonello calvetti/SS; 6-7, Courtesy Steve Brusatte; 10 (UP), Courtesy Steve Brusatte; 10 (LO), Jean-Michel Girard/SS; 11 (UP RT), Marques/SS; 11 (LO), Courtesy Steve Brusatte; 13 (UP), Spencer Platt/GI; 13 (LO), Universal Images Group North America LLC/DeAgostini/ASP; 14 (LO), Carlos Goldin/SCI; 15 (UP), Don Emmert/AFP/GI; 16, Stocktrek Images, Inc./ASP; 17 (UP), James Nesterwitz/ASP; 17 (CTR), John Weinstein/Field Museum Library/GI; 17 (LO), DM7/SS; 18 (UP), Sergey Krasovskiy/Stocktrek Images/SCI; 19, Kurt Miller/Stocktrek Images/GI; 20 (UP), FIMP/SS; 20 (LO), Lefteris Paupalakis/S; 21 (UP), Royal Tyrrell Museum; 22 (UP), Walter Myers/SCI; 22 (CTR), Sergey Krasovskiy/GI; 22 (LO), Mark Turner/ASP; 23 (CTR LE), Jan Sovak/Stocktrek Images, Inc./ASP; 24-25 (ALL), Courtesy Steve Brusatte; 27 (CTR), Walter Myers/Stocktrek Images/ASP; 27 (LO), Nobumichi Tamura; 28 (UP LE), Alice Turner/Stocktrek Images/GI; 28–29 (UP), Oxford Science Archive/Print Collector/GI; 29 (UP RT), Igor Karasi/SS; 31 (UP LE), MR1805/iStockphoto; 31 (UP RT), Royal Tyrrell Museum; 34 (UP), Courtesy Steve Brusatte; 34 (LO), Jean-Michel Girard/SS; 35 (UP LE), Courtesy Steve Brusatte; 35 (UP RT), Marques/SS; 36 (LO LE), Mikkel Juul Jensen/Bonnier Publications/SCI; 36–37 (UP), Stefan Schiessl/SCI; 37 (UP), All Canada Photos/ASP; 37 (LO RT), Dorling Kindersley/; 38, Yuriy Priymak/Stocktrek Images/SCI; 39 (LO LE), Igor Karasi/SS; 40 (UP RT), Courtesy Steve Brusatte; 41 (UP LE), Royal Tyrrell Museum; 41 (UP RT), Corbin17/ASP; 41 (LO), Jan Sovak/Stocktrek Images/ASP; 42 (UP), Rosa Jay/SS; 42 (LO), NPS/ASP; 44 (UP), Michael Rosskothen/SS; 44 (LO), Sergey Krasovskiy/Stocktrek Images/ASP; 45 (UP), Walter Myers/Stocktrek Images/ASP; 45 (LO LE), Amy Toensing/National Geographic Creative/ASP; 45 (LO RT), Mohamad Haghani/Stocktrek Images/ASP; 46 (LE), Robert Clark Photography; 46–47 (CTR), Richard Bizley/SCI; 48 (UP), Martin Shields/ASP; 49, Stocktrek Images, Inc./ASP; 50 (UP), MasPix/ASP; 50 (LO), Dorling Kindersley/GI; 51 (LO), Worakit Surijinda/SS; 52 (UP), Daniel Eskridge/Stocktrek Images/GI; 53 (UP), Martin Shields/ASP; 55 (UP), Zoonar/Elena Duvernay/ASP; 55 (LO), Dinoton/SS; 56 (LE), Art by James Havens 2017 @alaskapaleoproductions; 57 (UP), Mohamad Haghani/Stocktrek Images/ASP; 57 (LO), Sue Anne Zollinger/The Company of Biologists; 58 (UP LE), Alexander Koerner/GI; 58 (RT), milehightraveler/GI; 58 (LO LE), Tom Bean/ASP; 62 (UP), Courtesy Steve Brusatte; 62 (LO), Jean-Michel Girard/SS; 63 (UP LE), Courtesy Steve Brusatte; 63 (UP RT), Marques/SS; 63 (LO), Courtesy Steve Brusatte; 64 (UP), Courtesy Dr. Martin Lockley, University of Colorado; 64 (LO), Courtesy Dr. Xing Lida; 65 (UP), Mohamad Haghani/ASP; 66 (UP), Philip Brownlow/Stocktrek Images/ASP; 66 (LO), Courtesy Nature.com/Dr. Mary Higby Schweitzer; 67 (LO), DeAgostini/GI; 68 (UP), Mohamad Haghani/ASP; 69 (UP), José Antonio Peñas/SCI; 69 (LO), Jan Sovak/Media Bakery; 70 (UP), reptiles4all/SS; 70 (LO), Mogens Trolle/SS; 71, The Photo Researchers/GI; 72 (UP), stevegeer/iStockphoto; 72 (LO), Universal Images Group North America LLC/DeAgostini/ASP; 73 (UP), Ryan M. Bolton/SS; 74 (UP), Michael Gilday/ASP; 74 (LO), Francois Gohier/SCI; 75 (ALL), Courtesy Steve Brusatte; 76 (UP), Victor Fondevilla/Universitat Autònoma de Barcelona; 76 (CTR), Francois Gohier/SCI; 76 (LO), Millard H. Sharp/SCI; 77, Courtesy permanent collection of The Judith River Foundation/Children's Museum of Indianapolis via Creative Commons; 78 (UP), Nobumichi Tamura; 78 (LO LE), Chris Hellier/SCI; 79 (LE), Yuriy Priymak/Stocktrek Images/SCI; 79 (LO), O. Louis Mazzatenta/National Geographic/GI; 80 (LO), nik wheeler/ASP; 81, Alexander Koerner/GI; 82 (UP RT), Ryan M. Bolton/SS; 82 (LO LE), ajt/SS; 82 (LO RT), Boonchuay1970/SS; 83 (CTR), Colin Keates/Dorling Kindersley/Natural History Museum, London/SCI; 83 (LO LE), anaken2012/SS; 83 (LO RT), Ortis/SS; 86 (UP), Courtesy Steve Brusatte; 86 (LO), Jean-Michel Girard/SS; 87 (UP LE), Courtesy Steve Brusatte; 87 (UP RT), Marques/SS; 87 (LO), Courtesy Steve Brusatte; 88, Mark Garlick/Science Photo Library/ASP; 89 (UP), Detlev van Ravensway/SCI; 89 (LO), David Parker/SCI; 90 (UP), Richard Bizley/SCI; 90 (LO), Mark Garlick/Science Photo Library/GI; 91, Richard Bizley/SCI; 92 (UP), Aleksey Baskakov/Dreamstime; 93 (UP LE), Albert Russ/SS; 93 (UP RT), Colin Keates/Dorling Kindersley/SS; 93 (CTR), Sinclair Stammers/SS; 93 (LO), Pictorial Press Ltd/ASP; 94 (LO LE), Courtesy Steve Brusatte; 94 (LO RT), The Natural History Museum, London/ASP; 95 (UP), Science History Images/ASP; 96 (UP LE), The Natural History Museum, London/ASP; 96 (UP RT), Mark Garlick/Science Photo Library/ASP; 96 (CTR LE), Courtesy Library of Congress; 96 (LO), The Natural History Museum, London/ASP; 96 (LO LE), David Roland/ASP; 96 (LO RT), Leonello Calvetti/ASP; 97, George Rinhart/Corbis via GI; 98 (UP LE), Guido Martini/EyeEm/GI; 98 (UP RT), Jonathan Blair/Corbis Collection/GI; 98 (LO), Courtesy Rukwa Rift Basin Project; 99 (UP), O. Louis Mazzatenta/GI; 100–101, NG Maps; 102, paleontologia natural/SS; 103 (UP), Damian Kelly Photography; 103 (LO), Courtesy Darla Zelenitsky; 104 (UP), Joseph Nettis/SS; 104 (LO), Smithsonian Institute/SCI; 105 (UP), Frank Duenzl/picture-alliance/dpa/AP Images; 105 (LO), Ingo Schulz/imageBROKER/ASP; 106 (UP), Courtesy Steve Brusatte; 106 (LO LE), STR/AFP/GI; 106 (LO RT), Phil Degginger/ASP; 107 (toothbrush), Obak/SS; 107 (trowel), Thammasak Lek/SS; 107 (fork and spoon), Khongtham/SS; 107 (paintbrush), Seregam/SS; 107 (notebook), Mark Thiessen/NG Staff; 107 (pencil), Julia Ivantsova/SS; 107 (screwdriver), pchais/SS; 107 (hammer), Vrabelpeter1/SS; 107 (tape measure), Madlen/SS; 107 (chisel), rawf8/SS; 107 (water bottle), Odua Images/SS; 107 (kit), modustollens/SS

INDEX

To all of my teachers, from elementary school to graduate school, who fostered my love of learning and science. —SB

For every kid who has ever wanted to know MORE. —LN

Copyright © 2018 National Geographic Partners, LLC

Published by National Geographic Partners, LLC. All rights reserved. Reproduction of the whole or any part of the contents without written permission from the publisher is prohibited.

Since 1888, the National Geographic Society has funded more than 12,000 research, exploration, and preservation projects around the world. The Society receives funds from National Geographic Partners, LLC, funded in part by your purchase. A portion of the proceeds from this book supports this vital work. To learn more, visit natgeo.com/info.

NATIONAL GEOGRAPHIC and Yellow Border Design are trademarks of the National Geographic Society, used under license.

For more information, visit nationalgeographic.com, call 1-800-647-5463, or write to the following address:

National Geographic Partners
1145 17th Street N.W.
Washington, D.C. 20036-4688 U.S.A.

Visit us online at nationalgeographic.com/books

For librarians and teachers: ngchildrensbooks.org

More for kids from National Geographic:
natgeokids.com

For information about special discounts for bulk purchases, please contact National Geographic Books Special Sales: specialsales@natgeo.com

For rights or permissions inquiries, please contact National Geographic Books Subsidiary Rights: bookrights@natgeo.com

Designed by Girl Friday Productions

Hardcover ISBN: 978-1-4263-3140-4
Reinforced library binding ISBN: 978-1-4263-3141-1

Acknowledgments
A big thanks to all of my friends and colleagues who I have profiled in this book, most notably Tom Challands, Jon Hoad, Junchang Lü, Grzegorz Niedzwiedzki, and Tom Williamson and his sons Ryan and Taylor, as well as all of my colleagues around the world and my mentors (Paul Sereno, Mike Benton, and Mark Norell). I am particularly grateful to the National Geographic Society for funding my fieldwork hunting dinosaurs in Scotland. I am proud to be part of the family of National Geographic Explorers. And finally, thanks to Lela, Karen, and the team behind this book for making this such a fun project. —SB

Huge thanks to Girl Friday Productions and National Geographic for bringing me aboard this fun and fascinating project. — LN

The authors and publisher also wish to thank the book team: Shelby Lees, project editor; Kathryn Williams, editorial assistant; Amanda Larsen, art director; Sarah J. Mock, photo editor; Molly Reid, production editor; and Anne LeongSon, production assistant.

Printed in China
18/RRDS/1